Teaching Science Fact with Science Fiction

Teaching Science Fact with Science Fiction

GARY RAHAM

TEACHER IDEAS PRESS
Portsmouth, NH

Teacher Ideas Press
A division of Reed Elsevier Inc.
361 Hanover Street
Portsmouth, NH 03801-3912
www.teacherideaspress.com

Offices and agents throughout the world

The author and publisher wish to thank those who have generously given permission to
reprint borrowed material:

Excerpt from *Another Kind of Autumn* by Loren Eiseley. Published by Scribner, a division of Simon and
Schuster, Inc. Copyright © 1977 by the estate of Loren Eiseley. Reprinted by permission of the publisher.

Excerpt from *City* by Clifford D. Simak. Copyright © 1952, 1980 by Clifford D. Simack. Published by Ace
Books, Inc. Reprinted by permission of the Estate of Clifford D. Simack.

Excerpt from *The Cosmic Dancers* by Amit Goswami. Published by permission of the author.

Excerpt from *The Deep Times Diaries* by Gary Raham. Copyright © 2000 by Gary Raham. Reprinted by
permission of the author.

Excerpt from *Profiles of the Future* by Arthur C. Clarke. Published by Henry Holt. Reprinted by permission
of Scovil Chichak Galen, Inc.

Excerpt from *Dune* by Frank Herbert. Copyright © 1965 by Frank Herbert/Herbert Limited Partnership.
Published by Ace Books, Inc. Reprinted by permission of Herbert Limited Partnership.

Library of Congress Cataloging-in-Publication Data

Raham, Gary.
    Teaching science fact with science fiction / Gary Raham.
        p. cm.
    Includes bibliographical references.
    ISBN 1-56308-939-4
    1. Science—Study and teaching. 2. Science fiction in science
education. I. Title.
    Q147.R34 2004
    507'.1—dc22   2003027152

Editor: Suzanne Barchers
Production Coordinator: Angela Laughlin
Typesetter: Westchester Book Services
Cover design: Gary Raham
Manufacturing: Jamie Carter

Printed in the United States of America on acid-free paper

08 07 06 05 04   VP   1 2 3 4 5

Contents

Preface

Forgive me, but I've already made a few assumptions about you, the reader:

1. You are either a science teacher in some capacity or have a strong interest in science education.

2. You have at least a passing interest in science fiction.

If those two assumptions are correct, I also would expect you to sympathize with the view that nearly all mysteries ultimately yield to asking and answering (through experimentation) the proper series of questions. The premise that no mysteries should be "off limits" to questioning serves as a corollary to this attitude. Therein lies the excitement and fulfillment of scientific inquiry. Perhaps you are disheartened that so few people see science as an ongoing and creative process, but look upon it, at best, as a collection of facts and laws and may even equate it with the technology that others have created from its discoveries. You may yearn to ignite others with the enthusiasm that drew you to the study of science, but are struggling to find just the right way. I believe *Teaching Science Fact with Science Fiction* can help you in your search.

Science can seem to be a plodding exercise in methodical procedure and constant, critical thinking for those who can't appreciate the thrill of discovery that follows such efforts. Not everyone is suited to pursue science as an occupation. But science has utterly altered our view of the world and so rapidly increased our collective capacity to change the world that everyone needs to understand how it works and what it can and cannot do. That's where science fiction comes in. Science fiction tells stories. Human beings respond to stories as a way to learn. Good science fiction starts with a universe consistent with scientific discoveries and operating under natural laws as we understand them at the time, and it extrapolates futures we may or may not like—futures we can aim to build or strive to avoid. Most students will not become scientists, but all students will live their lives in a world where boundaries are defined by science and where tools are forged by the engineers and technicians who use science to create technology. Students should learn that science is not magic, but it is an amazingly powerful tool that, when used carefully and with some insight, can greatly enrich our lives.

Teaching Science Fact with Science Fiction provides upper-elementary through secondary teachers with specific suggestions for using the literature of science fiction (SF) to get students excited about science. To a lesser extent it provides hints for using SF in the media to accomplish the same ends. Story motivates learning. Once one is engaged in a story, pursuit of the knowledge that leads to understanding the story becomes an adventure instead of a chore.

The book begins by surveying the history of the scientific revolution over the last 500 years and the concurrent growth of a science fiction literature that takes the discoveries of science as a baseline. That literature transforms a tool for understanding nature into a kind of mythos that attempts to make sense of knowledge in human terms and provides warnings for misuse of that knowledge. Concrete suggestions and lesson plans serve as the heart of the book, exploring how specific SF works can provide leads into the physical, Earth, and life sciences, as well as interdisciplinary links with history and math. After reading Chapter 1, feel free to dip directly into those chapters (6 through 9) that deal specifically with your areas of expertise. Peruse Chapters 2 through 4 for an overview of how the science fiction you may want to use fits into the scientific understanding and social assumptions of the times. Chapter 5 provides the opportunity to compare and contrast science fiction in its various popular forms, including TV, film, short story, and Web manifestations.

Be sure and make use of the appendices as well. Appendix 1 provides lots of resources for keeping the facts and fiction straight in your own mind as well as the students'. Appendix 2 provides a summary of national science content standards. Appendix 3 summarizes all of the activities proposed in the book with suggestions for appropriate grade levels, and Appendix 4 offers samples of concrete lesson plans I have developed with classroom teachers.

I have taught science at the high school and intermediate level, and have written science fiction stories for adult markets and science fact articles for a variety of trade and educational publications. I have been privileged to work with talented teachers who have used my science fiction/science fact book, *The Deep Time Diaries,* in their science and English classrooms. I've seen how imaginative literature can transform student perceptions from indifference to excitement. As SF writer David Hartwell says in *Age of Wonder,* "You must understand that a constant desire for arousal, for that electric input that charges the 'wonder sense,' is what really hooks people on science fiction. . . ."

I hope you share my enthusiasm for this approach to teaching as you explore the resources in this book and use them to make your classroom an exciting place to be.

Acknowledgments

Many thanks to Suzanne Barchers, my editor, who provides splendid support and always seems to nudge my writing and organization into the most effective channels. Michael Blair, who has used science fiction to good effect in his own teaching, proved to be a valuable sounding board—along with some of his students—for early drafts of the book. Vicky Jordan believed in *The Deep Time Diaries* enough to incorporate it into her eighth-grade science curriculum and also read early drafts of this project. Science fiction writers Connie Willis and Wil McCarthy tried to keep me on track and keep the writing lively and interesting. Dick Scott kept an eye on the science content part of things. Of course, I take full responsibility for any errors or didacticism that may have slipped in despite their efforts.

Introduction

We live among the artifacts of scientific thinking and view the universe through a lens of inductive and deductive reasoning that has allowed us to glimpse vistas and understand natural laws undreamed of just a few centuries ago. We take much of this for granted, but shouldn't. Human beings don't take to scientific thinking easily. As Mr. Spock in the old *Star Trek* television series observed many times, human beings are highly illogical. They rely on emotion, prejudice, superstition, and intuition to make most day-to-day decisions. Loren Eiseley, in *The Man Who Saw through Time,* (Eiseley, 1973) (1), observed that "science among us is an *invented* cultural institution, an institution not present in all societies, and not one that may be counted upon to arise from human instinct."

When did this "invention" occur? The word "scientist" was not coined until 1840 (2) at a time when few people were actually making a full-time job exploring nature in a systematic way. The ancient Chinese may have observed a nova in the heavens as early as 1300 B.C. and had observed "Halley's" comet in 240 B.C. (Menzies, 2002), but modern science grew from Greek thought and observations. For a long time the Western world revered their knowledge and wisdom, but failed to absorb their questioning *attitude*. It wasn't until the late sixteenth and early seventeenth centuries that what we call the "Scientific Revolution" began to permeate Western thought and erode a long-established world view—a world view based on the preeminence of Spirit over matter. Galileo observed that philosophy is written in the language of mathematics and Newton demonstrated that premise with equations that tied heavenly motions to those of the matter that dominates our terrestrial experience.

The prerevolution world view was comforting: Humankind inhabited planet Earth at the center of God's creation. St. Thomas Aquinas, the thirteenth-century Dominican who tried to reconcile Greek rationalism and scripture, equated God with Aristotle's Prime Mover and suggested that Ptolemy's ordered firmament must consist of a series of nested, crystalline spheres turning about the Earth. The sun and stars occupied distant spheres, while the moon rode upon the innermost sphere. The world was changeable and imperfect below these celestial spheres, but the wisdom of the Greeks and the Word of God in the Bible provided sufficient guidelines to understand events as they unfolded (Suplee, 2000).

Imaginative literature in the early seventeenth century still reflected this world view. As Alexei and Cory Panshin point out in their book, *The World beyond the Hill* (Panshin and Panshin, 1989), Shakespeare could use witches, ghosts, and magic as serious plot elements in *Hamlet, Macbeth,* and *The Tempest* to capture that sense of transcendent wonder a reader craves in order to gain perspective on how the world works. Milton and Bunyan could deal with the old Heaven and Hell in *Paradise Lost* and *Pilgrim's Progress* for the same effect. "Spirit" provided the power and mystery in mythic literature. By the 1690s, such viewpoints had lost much of their plausibility—at least for the well educated. Social revolutions in England and France forced people to question the Divine Right of its kings and the Roman Catholic church's power declined sharply. People began questioning old assumptions and superstitions. They looked up at the heavens, scanned nature with a critical eye, and began noticing some discrepancies.

Copernicus, Galileo, and other astronomers blew the loudest wake-up call, announcing that the sun and not the Earth was at the center of things. Kepler discovered that planets travel in ellipses, not perfect circles, as they move about the sun. Naturalists of other persuasions discovered previously unknown, microscopic life in ponds, in dirt, and even in the scum between their teeth. Explorers found a host of undreamed-of plants and animals. People came awake to the notion that the Greeks didn't know everything after all and that nature could provide some interesting answers if you simply asked the proper questions. In 1605, Francis Bacon formalized this new world view in his book, *The Advancement of Learning* (Eiseley, 1973, p. 32). Bacon said: "This is the foundation of all, for we are not to imagine or suppose, but to *discover*, what nature does or may be made to do." Bacon, and many other thinkers, began to look upon the universe as a puzzle to be solved rather than a fixed stage that a person had to successfully traverse during his brief lifetime.

In short, the old spirit-based world view said: There are capricious forces in the universe we cannot hope to understand, so we must placate them—get them on our side. The new, rationalist/materialist viewpoint said: If we only knew all the rules of the game, we could explain any event and use the knowledge to our advantage. This latter view was generating exciting shifts in how people viewed the world and their place in it. Ultimately, this was reflected in a change in imaginative literature.

From utopian stories like *Gulliver's Travels* to experimental stories of mystery like *The Castle of Otranto,* to stories warning of human hubris like Mary Shelley's *Frankenstein,* writers began to develop a new mythos built around the accumulating discoveries of the scientific method. By the mid-1850s, Jules Verne had conceived the idea of "science romances" and penned *Journey to the Center of the Earth* (1864) and *From the Earth to the Moon* (1865) before writing *20,000 Leagues under the Sea* in 1869–70. H. G. Wells followed with *The Time Machine* (1895), and *The War of the Worlds* (1898) (Panshin and Panshin, 1989).

Hugo Gernsback, in the 1920s, used Wells, Verne, and Edgar Allan Poe as templates for a brand of fiction he called "scientifiction" in the magazine *Amazing Stories*. While that name didn't stick, his brand of fiction did, and reached a "Golden Age" by mid-century with John Campbell in the pages of *Astounding* and other pulp magazines. Novelists like Olaf Stapledon wove the wonders of science into heady narratives that spanned widening perceptions of space and time. Once the specialty of geeky young males, the genre has matured with the help of many fine women writers and fans. Though still "idea driven," much of modern science fiction is filled with good writing and believable characters. "Science fiction" or "speculative fiction" or just "SF" now comes in "hard" and "soft" varieties, the former having the strongest tradition of being true to scientific principles and discoveries while still maintaining that sense of wonder and excitement that you want to harness in your classrooms. Most of the titles referred to in this book come from this subgenre.

While science has wrought lasting and pervasive changes in our culture and our psyches over the last 500 years, its everyday practice—involving painstaking observations, experimentation, and peer review—can seem as exciting as watching a cheap screen saver for students attuned to processing information in "sound byte" increments. What I hope to give you with this book is a variety of literary and cinematic tools that will allow you to transmit some of the transcendent wonder science can reveal to those students who will use (or reject) science-based technology to forge our future. Science offers many possibilities, some grand and some highly dangerous. We all need to be able to understand enough science to distinguish it from the magic and superstition of earlier centuries. Today's student can and *must* learn both the laws of nature already revealed by scientists *and the scientific mode of thinking that will reveal new ones* to survive and prosper in a future of our collective making whose borders will be staked at the limits of our imaginations.

Science fiction can allow students to test those borders and, as several fictional starship captains have said, "boldly go where no one has gone before."

NOTES

(1) Eiseley wrote about the English philosopher Francis Bacon (1561–1626), who outlined the role of science and made it respectable. He served at the courts of Elizabeth I and James I. Bacon undoubtedly saw "opening night" for many of Shakespeare's plays. (In fact, some scholars have speculated he may have written some of them!) Francis Bacon aspired to know everything there was to know. He should not be confused with Roger Bacon (~1220–1292), an English scholar with similar aspirations and a shared love of rational thinking. Among Roger's radical notions was the idea that the Earth was round. In fact, Columbus quoted Roger Bacon in a letter to Ferdinand and Isabella of Spain (See Asimov, 1972, for details). Read more about both Bacons in Chapter 2.

(2) Refer to Panshin and Panshin, 1989, pages 38–40. Not long after science became worthy of being a full-time occupation, the writer William Wilson, who was familiar with the work of Jules Verne, suggested the term "Science-Fiction" for his kind of story, but it didn't catch on.

REFERENCES

Asimov, Isaac. *Asimov's Biographical Encyclopedia of Science and Technology*. New York: Avon Books, 1972.

Eiseley, Loren. *The Man Who Saw through Time*. New York: Charles Scribner's Sons, 1973.

Menzies, Gaven. *1421: The Year China Discovered America*. New York: William Morrow (Harper-Collins), 2002.

Panshin, Alexei, and Cory Panshin. *The World beyond the Hill*. Los Angeles: Jeremy P. Tarcher, 1989.

Suplee, Curt. *Milestones of Science*. Washington, DC: National Geographic, 2000.

CHAPTER 1

Using Fiction to Turn Kids On to Science

> *"These are the stories that the Dogs tell when the fires burn high and the wind is from the north. Then each family circle gathers at the hearthstone and the pups sit silently and listen and when the story's done they ask many questions:*
> *"What is Man?" they'll ask.*
> *Or perhaps: "What is a city?"*
> *Or: "What is a war?"*
> *"... In a family circle, many a storyteller has been forced to fall back on the ancient explanation that it is nothing but a story, there is no such thing as a Man or city, that one does not search for truth in a simple tale, but takes it for its pleasure and lets it go at that."*
> Clifford D. Simak, *City*

When I picked up Clifford Simak's *City* (Simak, 1952) as a teen and read the opening to the preface quoted above, chills crept up my neck. Cool. How had dogs inherited the Earth? What had happened to human beings? How far in the future did this all take place? I wanted to know. And more than that, I wanted to know how the author explained it all in the context of what I knew about how the world worked. Dogs telling stories around a campfire could have been pure fantasy, of course, but I didn't particularly care for fantasy. I knew I held a science fiction book in my hands and that somehow, the author was going to explain this future in a way that would make some logical sense to me. In essence, Clifford Simak had promised me four things:

1. He was going to tell me a good story. This is the key element. If the story doesn't grab you, why pay 35 cents (in 1952 dollars) and read 255 pages of small words on cheap paper?

2. He was going to show me a potential future. It might not be a future that would really happen, but it would be a future that *could* happen, with my present as the starting point.

3. He was going to make my life a little more exciting for the next few hours or days. He might even get me so wired that I'd want to learn more about genetic engineering or rocket science, or whatever he was going to tell me about.

4. He was going to reveal some Truth to me—an insight that would make me think "By gosh you're right, that's the way things are," or "I never thought of it *that* way before."

I contend that these four reasons are good reasons to use science fiction to teach science fact.

Figure 1.1. In Clifford Simak's *City,* dogs tell tales about their ancient masters who left for the stars.

TELLING A GOOD STORY

When you want to impress your own children with the dangers of driving you can (1) recite the latest statistics on death and mayhem as related to age, testosterone, and substance abuse or (2) tell that story about how you almost had a head-on collision trying to pass a semi the first time you crossed the Rockies during a spring snowstorm. Most of us choose the "When I was your age" option—instinctively, I suggest—because we know the attraction of placing familiar characters in danger and seeing how they get themselves out of it. Story comes naturally to us. Somewhere in the 2% difference in DNA between human beings and chimps (1) lie the secrets of language and grammar—the secrets of stringing sounds together in such a way that we can convey action, intent, and emotion, not only in the present, but also in the past and the future.

Even when languages die, we tend to make stories from visual images and artifacts left behind. When you look at those 20,000-year-old cave paintings from Altamira or Lascaux (2), don't you yearn to know the stories behind the hand prints and images of hunts and animal encounters concluded so long ago? Part of the allure of Simak's opening to *City* lies in its story-around-the-campfire beginning. How many generations of preliterate humans transmitted the truths and dangers of their existence in this way before the shiver up our collective spines became permanent? Did you look forward to storytelling time at school? How many "True Confessions" or mysteries did you read last year? Which commercials usually stick in your mind? The ones that tell amusing stories. Sometimes the stories are so good that we forget what they are selling. We pay attention to story first.

How best to impress someone with the dangers of two cultures clashing: (1) List the disastrous results of such meetings for human cultures over the past 4,000 years, or (2) tell the coming-of-age love story of a young girl from an advanced humanoid culture who tries to save two younger cultures at great risk to her own survival and happiness? The latter solution was chosen to great effect by Sylvia Louise Engdahl in her book, *Enchantress from the Stars* (Engdahl, 1970), a Newberry Honor Award book.

Elana stows away aboard her father's landing craft on a mission to Andrecia, a planet with a Medieval culture threatened by a spacefaring people who want to establish a colony there. Her father belongs to the Federation, an advanced society skilled in mental arts and dedicated to allowing the full development of all cultures. Somehow, they must avert the meeting of both "primitive cultures" (to avoid the subjugation, perhaps extinction, of the native Andrecian culture) without revealing themselves for what they are. Elana anticipates taking the Federation oath, but sneaks aboard the landing craft to be close to her friend, Evrick, on his first mission. When the only female member of the team dies, Elana is pressed prematurely into service. In the process of working with a clever woodcutter, Georyn, from the native culture to give him the "magic" he needs to slay the mechanical "dragon" of the spacefaring culture, she falls in love with her "student" and must make some difficult decisions in order for the Federation's mission to succeed.

Such an engaging story allows us to live Elana's mistakes, share her prejudices and disillusionments, exult in her successes, and *generalize* from dramatic, if fictional, specifics to broader philosophies of conduct distilled from the bare facts of human history. Here we get to become anthropologists of some distant future and examine some of our own assumptions and see if they are wanting. (Refer to Chapter 9 for an activity to try in the classroom based on this book or its sequel, *The Far Side of Evil* [1972]).

TRYING OUT ALTERNATE FUTURES

Trial and error governs the lives of simple-minded creatures. Worms crawl away from noxious chemicals. Protozoans bump into barriers and change directions until they find a way around an obstacle. More complex animals can learn from what they do. Birds begin to avoid brightly colored insects because they get sick whenever they eat one. Dogs learn tricks in order to earn a treat or a pat on the head. Human beings have carried the process to another level. We don't always have to physically do something to explore the consequences of an act. We are able to *imagine* a set of activities and—based partly on personal experience, and partly on the *stories* we've been told—visualize what might occur, given a certain set of initial conditions. Stories can serve as a way to explore actions with our mind before jumping off the cliff of experience. Science fiction stories can allow us to explore entire alternate timelines.

It's hard to know if post-Holocaust stories like *On the Beach* (Shute, 1957) or *Dr. Strangelove* (Dir. Stanley Kubrick, 1963) have helped us avert a nuclear disaster to this point in our history, but it would not be surprising. Such tales make it easier for us to place ourselves into a possible future and vicariously experience the implications of some discovery or event. *The Andromeda Strain* (Crichton, 1969) dramatized first contact with a fundamentally different kind of microscopic life at a time when we became more active in exploring the moon and neighboring planets. Since the discovery that the Yucatan peninsula of Mexico was whacked by space debris 65 million years ago in what was probably the final blow to dinosaurian life on Earth (3), movie audiences have been bombarded with movies like *Deep Impact* (1998). Astronomer and science popularizer Carl Sagan proposed that hydrogen bombs could mirror the effects of an asteroid impact by cooling the climate for an extended period of time. At least one *Star Trek Voyager* episode used such a "nuclear winter" scenario as a plot element.

Modern SF writers exploit the implications of discoveries in almost every field of science. Greg Bear, author of *Darwin's Radio* (1999), uses findings from molecular and evolutionary biology to weave a fascinating story to show how the next stage in human evolution might manifest itself. "Rocket scientist" and writer Wil McCarthy describes a future in *The Collapsium* (2000) made possible by harnessing superdense matter to build constructs that can warp space and time—and destroy stars, if you're not careful. (See Chapter 6.) Arthur C. Clarke, credited for predicting the Earth-orbiting satellite, continues to explore unusual technological possibilities with his geosynchronous "space elevator" concept that might allow relatively easy transportation between Earth and a space station in orbit about the Earth (4).

INSPIRATION TO CREATE THE FUTURE YOU WANT

Several generations of scientists have grown up reading science fiction. One of the early nuclear submarines bore the name *Nautilus* in honor of Captain Nemo's ship in *20,000 Leagues under the Sea*. Many aerospace engineers were the biggest fans of the original *Star Trek* with Captain Kirk and crew sailing the *Enterprise* through deep space. Consequently, it's no surprise that Congress was receptive to fans who urged that the first Space Shuttle Orbiter be named *Enterprise* instead of *Constitution* (5). The robots used in modern manufacturing don't possess the autonomy and intelligence of the robots in Isaac Asimov's *I, Robot* (1950) story collection, but they may owe their invention to some of the *possibilities* he imagineered with his fiction.

A number of scientists not only read SF, they write it as well. I've already mentioned "rocket scientist" Wil McCarthy and engineer Arthur C. Clarke. A small sampling of some others includes Fred Hoyle, Gene Wolfe, John Cramer, Carl Sagan, Joan Slonczewski, Robert L. Forward, David Brin, Gregory Benford, and Donald Kingsbury. "Despite this connection between science and sf," says Kathryn Cramer in an introduction to *The Ascent of Wonder* (Hartwell and Cramer, 1994), "the nature of this connection remains largely unexplored."

I mentioned in the introduction that much of the SF I will discuss in conjunction with teaching science is the "hard" variety. Hard in this case doesn't mean difficult, but a brand of science fiction that is true to scientific fact as understood at the time of writing. SF writer and editor David Hartwell says, "The attitude that underpins science fiction is that there is a reality beyond appearances which is knowable through science" (Hartwell and Cramer, 1994). The variety known as hard science fiction "emphasizes the rigorous nature of our relation to this reality behind experience." The writers and fans of hard SF share a kind of "cross talk" not unlike the peer review that scientists experience in their disciplines. A writer who violates known scientific principles without explanation would quickly lose his audience. Writers and readers get ample opportunity to share views and ideas in a variety of forums, including conventions, magazines, and "e-zines." Perhaps it's not surprising that potential scientists can be inspired by creative writers with a similar, deterministic mind set.

GENERATING THOSE SCIENCE-BASED EPIPHANIES

People want to be thrilled, inspired, and awed. They want to transcend the borders of their job, the realities of washing clothes and mowing lawns, the boring routines of schoolwork. But they want to do so in a way that makes sense to them—in a way that is consistent with their beliefs and views about how the world works. Every culture tends to create a "mythic literature," to not only explain their beliefs but provide ways to transcend tedium and imbue mere knowledge with meaning.

In the early fourteenth century, at the beginning of what we call the Little Ice Age, weather took a turn for the worse in Western Europe. Wet summers and severe storms ruined crops. Cold winters killed peasants already weakened by famine and disease. Why? It was obvious to most people: God was mad at them for some reason. People flocked to their churches and asked for guidance. The churches performed complex rogation ceremonies to pray for divine intervention (Fagin, 2000, p. 42). As Alexei and Cory Panshin point out in their book *The World beyond the Hill,* "The transcendent symbols of ancient myth were all grounded in a fundamental belief in the existence of *spirit,* as distinct from *matter*" (Panshin and Panshin, 1989, p. 7). While there was a connection between the two, spirit represented more powerful and enduring forces. Spirit in the form of God, saints, wizards, or witches could be counted on to inspire action, explain misfortune, or at least teach the young how to appease the angry forces of nature.

By the seventeenth century things had substantially changed—at least among intellectuals. Men with a rational-materialistic turn of mind, like Bacon, Kepler, Galileo, and Descartes, believed that objective examination of nature should prevail over mysticism (6). For many, old spirit-based stories lost their power to awe and inspire. For nearly a century there was little to replace them. Then, in 1764, Sir Horace Walpole (7) wrote *The Castle of Otranto,* inspired by a dream. Unsure of its reception, he wrote it as if it were an "old tale retold," so its "miraculous" elements could be explained away. The ghost of a Crusader in the form of a disembodied helmet, for example, played a key role in the book. But after it became a big hit, Walpole explained that he had intended to blend the miraculous and the reasonable all along, so that while dreams, visions, necromancy, and so forth were elements in the story, his characters acted "according to the rules of probability" (Panshin and Panshin, 1989, p. 15). At any rate, this book is now considered the basis for a host of modern story forms including the novel, the Gothic romance, the horror story, mystery, heroic fantasy, and modern SF.

And modern SF is considered—at least by some of its practitioners—to be the rationally based mythos that can awe and inspire because it is grounded in the natural rules of order as revealed through scientific investigation. The Panshins say (p. 17), "Here marvelous power displays itself everywhere, there are superior beings to be encountered, and we may undergo experiences that village knowledge (everyday experience) cannot encompass." Modern science has shown that the universe is not only breathtakingly large and awe-inspiring, but impersonal and dangerous as well. In fact, as long as humanity lives on one fragile planet, our sun could burp one day and we would all be fried, no matter how unique and clever we are. David Hartwell believes that science fiction's ultimate goal is nothing less than to find a way around humanity's ultimate extinction, at least within the lifetime of the known universe.

Science fiction thus provides stories of grand scope, with rational heroes, who optimistically seek survival and fulfillment against a ruthless, but beautiful and complex universe. Sounds like a modern mythos to me—and a great way to introduce science to kids.

IS SCIENCE FICTION "HEATHEN" LITERATURE?

Will science fiction literature alienate the religious in your classroom? Is it antireligion? Because science fiction sometimes attempts to "explain" religious phenomena in rational terms, and because SF literature taps heavily into that sense of wonder that may be shared by those who experience religious awe, it can seem to invade religious belief systems for some students. It's beyond the scope of this book to go into great detail in this area, but the short answers are "maybe" and "not particularly." Some students with fundamentalist backgrounds may take exception to some science fiction works. And the authors of science fiction write from a variety of backgrounds, both religious and purely secular, so it's unwise to make generalizations, but SF, like science, need not directly confront religious belief.

The late Stephen Jay Gould in *Rocks of Ages* (1999) proposes that science and religion occupy "non-overlapping magisteria" (NOMAs) that allow science and religion to peacefully coexist in their separate spheres of influence. Chet Raymo in *Skeptics and True Believers* (1998) says that we can and must build bridges between science and religion because they can mutually reinforce the way we experience the world. "Miracles are explainable," he says; "it is the explanations that are miraculous." It's a loss to our culture that the dialogue between science and religion isn't better, because well-meaning people on school boards sometimes set these human endeavors against one another instead of allowing each to address its particular strengths.

Religion is far older than science, of course, so science did colonize some of the territory formerly held by religion. You will see this in the next chapter, where we time travel a bit and explore the history of science over the last 500 years. We will also see how speculative literature evolved to reflect changing perceptions of the natural world that science brought about. This should provide you with an historical framework that will enrich your choices when you set out to select just the right story to launch your students into their next science lessons.

NOTES

(1) Recent sequencing of DNA from various organisms has shown Earth life to be quite conservative and resourceful. Not only do we share 98% of our DNA with chimps, we share 50% of the genes in the bananas they like to eat.

(2) The caves in Altamira, Spain, and Lascaux, France, are some of the first found and the most widely known. Cave paintings found in Chauvet, France, have been radio-carbon-dated at more than 30,000 years.

(3) This theory, controversial during the 1980s, but well established today after a number of tests and the discovery of a probable crater, is described dramatically by one of its proponents, Walter Alvarez, in *T. Rex and the Crater of Doom,* 1997.

(4) *Fountains of Paradise* (1980) won the Hugo for best novel in that year and describes the construction on Earth of a space elevator 36,000 km high. Arthur C. Clarke has remained creative and innovative over a long career. (See Chapters 9 and 10.)

(5) *Enterprise* never flew in space but served to test approach and landing systems, during both ground and flight tests. Astronaut crews landed the 150,000-pound unpowered craft five times. In 1985 it became part of the Smithsonian's collection.

(6) This is very much a generalization, of course, as witnessed even today by widespread beliefs in astrology, for example, by apparently well-educated people.

(7) Sir Horace Walpole (1717–1797) was an English writer best known for letters that dealt with party politics, foreign affairs, art, literature, and gossip of the day. He was the son of Sir Robert

Walpole (1676–1745), considered by some (though not by him) to be England's first Prime Minister during the reign of George I.

REFERENCES

Asimov, Isaac. *I, Robot.* New York: Signet Books, 1950.

Bear, Greg. *Darwin's Radio.* New York: Del Rey (Ballantine Publishing Group), 1999.

Crichton, Michael. *The Andromeda Strain.* New York: Knopf, 1969.

Dr. Strangelove or: How I Learned to Stop Worrying and Love the Bomb. Dir. Stanley Kubrick. Hawk/Columbia, 1963.

Engdahl, Sylvia Louise. *Enchantress from the Stars* (1970). New York: Walker & Co., 2001.

Engdahl, Sylvia Louise. *The Far Side of Evil.* New York: Atheneum, 1972.

Fagin, Brian. *The Little Ice Age: How Climate Made History, 1300–1850.* New York: Basic Books, 2000.

Gould, Stephen Jay. *Rocks of Ages: Science and Religion in the Fullness of Life.* New York: Ballantine Publishing Group, 1999.

Hartwell, David G., and Kathryn Cramer. *The Ascent of Wonder: The Evolution of Hard SF.* New York: TOR, 1994.

McCarthy, Wil. *The Collapsium.* New York: Del Ray (Ballantine Publishing Group), 2000.

Panshin, Alexei, and Cory Panshin. *The World beyond the Hill: Science Fiction and the Quest for Transcendence.* Los Angeles: Jeremy P. Tarcher, 1989.

Raymo, Chet. *Skeptics and True Believers.* New York: Walker & Co., 1998.

Shute, Nevil. *On the Beach.* New York: Bantam Books, 1957.

Simak, Clifford D. *City.* New York: Ace Books, 1952.

Verne, Jules. *20,000 Leagues under the Sea* (1872). Chicago: Children's Press, 1968.

ADDITIONAL READING

Alvarez, Walter. *T. Rex and the Crater of Doom.* Princeton, NJ: Princeton University Press, 1997.

Chauvet, Jean-Marie, Eliette Brunel Deschamps, and Hillaire Christian. *Dawn of Art: The Chauvet Cave.* London: Thames and Hudson Ltd.; New York: Harry N. Abrams, 1996.

Ridley, Matt. *Genome: The Autobiography of a Species in 23 Chapters.* New York: HarperCollins, 1999.

Ridley, Matt. "The Year of the Genome" in *Discover* 22, no. 1, January 2001: 50–53.

CHAPTER 2

The Origins of Science and Science Fiction: Serendipity and Genius

"If I have seen further it has only been by standing on the shoulders of giants."
Isaac Newton in a letter to Robert Hooke, 1675 (1)

Think of the last 100,000 years of human history (2) as a 500-page book—a heavy tome you may have had on your shelf for years, but never quite got around to reading. On a sleepy Sunday you pick it up, with the intent of learning something about the history of science. You turn the cover expectantly, and, to your dismay, discover that the pages are blank.

Well, not quite.

A few images turn up here and there: mostly pictures of bone fragments from old dead relatives. Sometimes you find images of stone, sharpened, used, and then lost or discarded. On page 350 you start to find some interesting pictures actually drawn by some more old dead relatives: elegant images of animals caught in motion, meant to be viewed in a ceremony of revelation or empowerment. On page 450 you find pictures of stone tablets etched with ciphers buried in the ruins of permanent settlements. On page 475 some text appears, revealing fragments of personal lives not unlike your own. Page 485 chronicles the first recorded eclipse of the sun in China. Beginning on page 489, you learn a few interesting thoughts recorded by Aristotle and other clever warrior-citizen-philosophers. Page 494 records a religious treatise, the Bible, in its entirety, and finally, in the middle of page 497, the musings of Copernicus strike a familiar chord: we can learn to judge reality through observation and experiment.

Two and half pages: a quick read in a long book.

The history of science stretches back only 500 years, yet it represents a revolution in the way of thinking about ourselves and how we interpret the rest of nature so profound that it has given us an unprecedented control of the world around us and altered, in an eyeblink, patterns of human existence that repeated unchanged for millennia. One is tempted to ask: why didn't someone think about this system of observation and experimentation before? Too few people to make a quorum? Not enough leisure time? Maybe. Just how improbable is the "scientific revolution" and the civilization that is willing and able to support it? And for Heaven's sake, why make up fictional stories about this problem-solving process?

The origins of both science and the imaginative literature that it spawned seem rooted in an equal mix of serendipity and genius, combined with a measure of good fortune. As you will see (especially in Chapter 9), this curious history provides all sorts of "what if?" opportunities for SF writers, not to mention teachers. Join me in a brief tour of these pivotal events—or jump directly to Chapter 6, if you are eager to begin with some specific classroom activities.

GREEK RATIONALISM

The mysteries of nature cry out for answers. We tremble before powers greater than ourselves; before beauty and complexity beyond individual understanding; before the wonder of birth and the fear of death. Great thinkers from all ages have looked around themselves and thought: This *creation* that we see must be the result of unseen powers beyond our control. Natural leaders, visionaries certain in their convictions, then proceed to found religions built on a belief in spirit and a formula of prayer designed to navigate believers through the uncertain waters of existence. Another subset of great thinkers look around themselves and observe that certain actions bring certain results. They believe in their senses and what those senses reveal about the world. Natural leaders and visionaries empower themselves to decide between cause and effect and to identify forces and how to control them. Spiritualism and rationalism seem to ebb and flow like the tides. The vast majority of us hang somewhere in the middle of things, trusting to our senses in most matters, but suspecting that God has set things in motion.

Greek civilization spawned a form of rationalism that underpins Western civilization and the rise of science. Aristotle (384–322 B.C.), a cerebral sort of fellow born to the court physician at Stagira in the Greek colony on Chaldice, founded an influential school (the Lyceum) in Athens in 335 B.C. that taught "all material things could be analyzed in terms of their matter and their form, and form constituted their essence" (3).

Much of Aristotle's notions came from Plato's (428–348 B.C.) dialogues. Plato turned away from a career in politics (or maybe poetry) after listening for many years to the oral teachings of an aging Socrates (470–399 B.C.) and being appalled at his execution by the State on specious charges of heresy. Socrates, as a middle-aged citizen-soldier of Athens in the Battle of Delium in 424 B.C., nearly got himself killed by a Theban cavalryman. Did the fate of modern science hinge on luck and bad swordsmanship? Greek thought, including Aristotle's, was later saved and translated by al-Mamun (786–833) in the House of Knowledge in Baghdad. What if Mamun the Great had never come to power, or there had been a fire . . . ? Perhaps some other concatenation of events would have saved Greek ideas for Thomas Aquinas, who made rationalism acceptable to the Catholic church. Perhaps not (4).

COPERNICUS AND A NEW SET OF STANDARDS

Let's Just Move the Earth

Nicolaus Copernicus (1473–1543) lived in heady times. While Copernicus was in his second year of college at Krakow University in Poland, Columbus sailed the blue ocean and discovered the Americas (5). If Copernicus had wanderlust, we don't know of it, but Columbus' voyage, like the moon landing in my generation, must have generated a certain sense of awe and appreciation for frontiers yet to be explored. We do know that Copernicus was fascinated by mathematics and astronomy and spent the fairly large sums necessary to acquire some personal volumes on those subjects. Like other scholars since, he scribbled notes in the margins as he read. One good idea often begets another.

Nicolaus finished his studies, and pleased his wealthy merchant father by becoming a doctor. He landed a secure, civil-servant position with an uncle in Warmia, a small feudal holding of the Catholic church in Poland. Nicolaus didn't neglect his hobbies and dreams, however. He studied the stars and planets and began a journey that would have been the envy of Columbus, had he known where it would ultimately lead.

Two astronomical problems fascinated Copernicus as they had other keen observers of the heavens: Why did some of the planets, particularly Mars and Jupiter, vary in brightness? And did Ptolemy's complicated series of epicycles really explain the phenomenon of retrograde motion?

Copernicus realized that Ptolemy's entire scheme would become much less complicated if the sun, and not the Earth, were at the center of the solar system. "For who would place this lamp of a most beautiful temple in a better place?" (Suplee, 2000). And if the Earth were also turning on its own axis, that would explain the apparent motion of planets from east to west across the sky. Copernicus decided that Mercury and Venus were closer to the sun because they always appeared close to the sun in the sky. The retrograde motions of Jupiter, Mars, and Saturn could be explained if they orbited the sun at a greater distance than Earth. That way the Earth, moving in a faster, inner orbit, would overtake the outer planets at some point making their motion across the sky seem to slow down and even reverse direction part of the time. Not only that, the planets would appear brighter when they were closer and fainter when they were farther away. Both problems could be solved just by moving the Earth!

Other people had considered a sun-centered solar system. But the yardstick for the acceptability of an idea had always been: how well does it conform with history and tradition? The true genius of Copernicus was insisting on a new yardstick: *How well does this idea conform to what I actually observe in nature and how elegantly does it please the mind?* This new measure for describing nature serves as the keystone for the scientific revolution (Neyman, 1974).

If You Can Move the Earth Then . . .

Copernicus' new yardstick struck a sympathetic chord with other keen observers of the time. Johannes Kepler (1571–1630), a mathematical "whiz kid" of his day, labored over the meticulous celestial observations of his mentor, Tycho Brahe (1546–1601), for six years trying to iron out some lingering problems with Copernicus' work. The solution finally came to him: "It seemed as if I awoke from sleep and saw a new light break on me," Kepler said (Suplee, 2000). The planets don't travel around the sun in perfect circles, but in slightly "squashed" circles, or ellipses. An ellipse is a geometrical figure with two foci (instead of one center, like a circle) and the sun always occupies one of those foci (Kepler's First Law). Moreover, a line connecting the sun and a planet sweeps out equal areas in a given time (Kepler's Second Law), which allows for precise predictions of planetary speed. Kepler's Third Law states that the time taken by any given planet to orbit the sun, when squared, is proportional to its average distance from the sun cubed. Theories leading to testable predictions are also a hallmark of science. Without them a theory has no scientific value.

Galileo (1564–1642) improved greatly on the design of refracting telescopes and made brilliant observations of the heavens. He discovered sunspots and observed that the sun itself must be turning on its axis. He described the terrain of the moon in detail, observed the phases of Venus, discovered that Jupiter had moons of its own, and found numerous, previously unseen stars.

Observe carefully, make a prediction based on those observations (hypothesize), and test your prediction in a controlled way. Men with a curious turn of mind found that mysteries fell to these techniques. But learned men weren't quite sure what to make of these inventive observers and craftsmen. Some, after all, came from quite humble circumstances. What the practitioners of this investigative "scientific method" needed at this point was a good PR man. Francis Bacon (1561–1626) filled the bill.

The Man Who Saw through Time

Francis Bacon, essentially an opportunistic politician in the courts of Elizabeth I and James I in England, became fascinated by what we would call the scientific approach to problem solving. He said that Aristotle's deductive method of reasoning (establishing certain premises and deducing consequences) was fine for mathematics, but insufficient for science. For the latter you must be able to induce general principles by making precise observations. In 1605 he published his ideas in *The Advancement of Learning*. Loren Eiseley praised Bacon's vision in his own book, *The Man Who Saw through Time* (Eiseley, 1973). "Yet it is this man," says Eiseley, "who first fully visualized in all its splendor the 'invention of inventions'—the experimental method which would unlock the riches of the modern world."

Bacon, well educated and articulate, gave science respectability among the intellectuals of Elizabethan England, who might otherwise have considered Leeuwenhoek, Galileo, and many of the other innovative observers mere tinkerers or hobbyists. Science became so fashionable, in fact, that it eventually led to a community of investigators and philosophers that became the Royal Society of London. Ironically, Bacon didn't much care for Copernicus' ideas, especially the notion of the Earth actually speeding through space, and he was more of an armchair scientist than an actual experimentalist himself, although a field observation ultimately led to his death. While he was driving home in his carriage one chilly day in 1626, the notion occurred to him that cold temperatures might slow the putrefaction of meat. He bought a chicken and stuffed it with snow, intending to test the idea (Asimov, 1972). Apparently the adventure took too much time, because he caught a chill, which turned to bronchitis, and he died shortly thereafter.

The First Science Fiction Story?

Johannes Kepler, the brilliant mathematician who tidied up planetary motions, may also be credited with the first true science fiction story (Asimov, 1972). Kepler wrote a story (published after his death) called "Somnium" about a man who traveled to the surface of the moon in a dream. The details of lunar topography were true to the observations of Galileo—and perhaps to Kepler's own observations, as Galileo, at some point, had sent him one of his refracting telescopes. Kepler's manuscripts were purchased by Catherine II over a century after his death and now reside in Russia.

Figure 2.1. Sir Isaac Newton brought the motion of heavenly bodies within the realm of Earth-based mathematics.

NEWTON'S GRAND SYNTHESIS

A Genius Leads the Way

Sir Isaac Newton (1642–1727), described by some as the greatest intellect who ever lived, barely survived a premature birth. He was a strange, curious, inventive child, turned inward by temperament and circumstance. An uncle who was a member at Trinity College in Cambridge convinced his reluctant mother that Newton should pursue an academic career. Newton graduated from Cambridge in 1665, having figured out by this time the binomial theorem of mathematics $[(a+b)^2 = a^2 + 2ab + b^2]$. His unique talents began to surface this same year after he retreated to his mother's farm to escape the plague in London. In a burst of creative insight he worked out the basics of calculus (discovered independently by Gottfried Leibniz [1646–1716])—a quantitative way to summarize motion at any point through time and space—and recognized in an epiphany, during the fall of an apple, that the forces that acted on Earth were identical to those that acted on the moon and planets.

In 1668 Newton invented an elegant reflecting telescope, which bounced light off a parabolic mirror, avoided the chromatic aberration problems of refracting telescopes, and allowed the user to observe without getting in the path of incoming light. This concrete accomplishment alone provided immediate entry into the Royal Society.

In 1687 he published *Principia Mathematica* (at the urging and with the financial support of Edmund Halley), which, in a simple and elegant way, provided the mathematical underpinning for Kepler's Laws and Galileo's observations of heavenly motions: $F = Gm_1 m_2/d^2$. The force of attraction (F) between two masses (m_1 and m_2) is inversely proportional to the square of the distance (d) between them. G is a gravitational constant that was precisely determined by Cavendish a century later. This discovery put Newton a notch above Aristotle in the mind of intellectuals, who recognized that this equation revealed a fundamental truth about matter and force in the universe.

In 1704 Newton published *Optiks,* a book that outlined his theories of light. He believed light consisted of particles (only partly true, as it turned out) and that refracting telescopes would always be flawed because of chromatic aberration—the prism-like splitting of white light into colors near the edges of lenses (this problem was solved shortly after his death).

Newton was far from perfect. He went down blind alleys in chemistry trying to make gold, he speculated endlessly on certain mystical passages in the Bible, and he engaged in petulant arguments with Robert Hooke (1635–1702) and other peers. But he gave the world this: a sense that the workings of the universe could be divined, as it were, by reason. Alexander Pope wrote:

> Nature and Nature's laws lay hid in night:
> God said, Let Newton be, and all was light. (Asimov, 1972)

Would history have shaped another man to inspire an "Age of Reason," or would science have faltered without Newton's particular genius?

The Beginnings of the Age of Reason

Newton lay at the center of a movement that invited new discoveries regarding universal operating principles. His contemporaries included Robert Boyle (1627–1691), who discovered the relationship between pressure and volume in gases; Olaus Romer (1644–1710), who determined that light travels at a finite speed; and Edmund Halley (1656–1743), who developed a theory of comets and successfully predicted the return of the comet now named after him. Robert Hooke proposed a wave theory of light that put him at odds with Newton (6), but he also invented a compound microscope that allowed him to see new microscopic worlds, revealed in his book *Micrographia* (1665). Marcello Malpighi (1628–1694) discovered blood capillaries, which supported William Harvey's theory of blood circulation. Nicolaus Steno (1638–1686) and Robert Hooke both recognized fossils as the petrified remains of once-living creatures (Suplee, 2000).

Discoveries piled on discoveries, making communication between researchers more difficult. Two institutions to aid scientific communication got their start at this time. One, already mentioned in connection with Francis Bacon, was the Royal Society of London for the Promotion of Natural Knowledge, chartered by the King in 1662. The society's journal, *Philosophical Transactions,* accepted work from men of all social standings doing exciting work, such as Antony van Leeuwenhoek (1632–1723), the janitor/lens grinder from Holland who discovered the first protozoa and made more careful observations of capillaries than their discoverer, Malpighi. The Academy of Sciences began in Paris in 1666. Its publication, *Memoires,* represents the second venerable venue for evaluating new scientific discoveries. Both organizations created acceptable standards of quality, disseminated information among members, and established the priority of discovery between people working in the same areas.

APPLYING REASON: A NEW WORLD VIEW

Reason and Revolution

It may seem contradictory that a period of time called the Age of Reason should be so unruly, but the attitude of scientific rationalism eroded old assumptions that lay at the heart of social order. Kings lost divine sanctions. The well-born and noble, if they cheated, lied, and/or committed stupid acts, lost the automatic deference they had always been paid. And when social order decayed, even the undeserving fell in the crossfire. Such was the case for Antoine Lavoisier (1743–1794), a brilliant Frenchman who became a victim of the French Revolution.

Lavoisier has been lauded as the "Father of Modern Chemistry" and the "Newton of Chemistry" for good reason (Asimov, 1972):

- He hammered away at the importance of precise measurements when trying to unravel natural laws. For example, he carried out meticulous measurements to show that the sediment formed in a flask of boiling water was actually eroded particles of glass and not some new substance created by the transformation of water.

- He debunked the long-held idea that combustible objects contained a fluid substance called phlogiston that was consumed in the burning process. He was able to show that material burned in sealed containers with air present actually gained weight, but wouldn't burn at all without air. Something in the air was important for combustion. (Joseph Priestley [1733–1804] helped him realize that that substance was a gaseous element, later named oxygen.)

- His precise measurements allowed him to define the Law of Conservation of Mass: mass is neither lost nor gained in a chemical reaction, just moved from one reactant to the other.

- He standardized the naming of chemicals still used today in his *Methods of Chemical Nomenclature* (1787).

- He wrote what amounts to the first chemical textbook—*Elementary Treatise on Chemistry* (1789)—in which he stated his conservation law clearly, revived the concept of the chemical element, and listed all the elements known at the time.

But Lavoisier made two social mistakes: He invested in a tax-collecting company (and married the daughter of the owner) hired by the French government that cheated the French peasantry, and he denied entry of Jean Paul Marat to the French Academy of Sciences. Marat later became a revolutionary radical, remembered the slight, and targeted Lavoisier. When Lavoisier protested to the arresting soldier that he was a scientist and not a "tax farmer," the soldier said, "The Republic has no need of scientists." Lavoisier lost his head on the guillotine in 1794, although two years later the regretful French were making busts of that same head.

Reason and Nature

The Age of Reason also ultimately gave the fledgling United States its only true scientist/president in the form of Thomas Jefferson (1743–1826). Jefferson became intrigued by fossils, which had been collected by gentlemen for many years as curious, "formed" objects thought to be crafted by God and placed in the Earth. First Robert Hooke and Nicolaus Steno, later William Smith (1769–1839) and others realized fossils represented the remains of once-living creatures. Disturbing to many, most of these creatures seemed to have no living counterparts—a fact that seemed to deny the perfection and permanence of divine creation. Jefferson studied the remains of mammoths and mastodons in France and in North America, and discovered the giant claw of a beast later identified as a giant ground sloth. At the time, Jefferson had hopes that some of these animals still lived in America's unexplored interior.

Discoveries of the late eighteenth and early nineteenth centuries empowered human beings to think in new ways and glimpse grand horizons of possibility—both in control of nature and toward more perfect societies. James Watt (1736–1819) perfected the steam engine, Ben Franklin (1706–1790) discovered that lightning was a form of electricity, John Dalton (1766–1844) proposed the atomic theory,

Figure 2.2. Thomas Jefferson appreciated the power of reason and searched for strange beasts in the American wilderness that could explain the strange fossils he and others were discovering.

Alessandro Volta (1745–1827) impressed Napoleon (and others) with the electric battery, William Smith outlined his theory of geological stratigraphy, and Charles Lyell (1797–1875) published his *Principles of Geology*. In Italy, Luigi Galvani performed experiments showing that electricity could make unattached frog legs twitch, implying that nerve conduction was somehow electrical in nature. Some of his studies became so popular that when a person is inspired or "shocked" into action we say he or she is "galvanized"—a term we will shortly note in connection with some early science fiction.

Early Imaginative Literature: Fear and Wonder

Men and Monsters

Imaginative literature took a while to find a place among all the "reasonableness" of the Age of Reason. Who could take seriously ghosts and spirits as elements of mystery and power when skeptics could laugh and say, "There's no such thing!" The fantastical elements in *Gulliver's Travels* served the purposes of satire. Utopian stories sketched the workings of "perfected societies" in more of a tour guide fashion.

As mentioned in Chapter 1, Sir Horace Walpole, member of the British Parliament and son of a Prime Minister, took up the challenge, though in a rather timid way (until it became popular), with *The Castle of Otranto,* his only novel (Panshin and Panshin, 1989, p. 15). Walpole seemed more secure with his essays, verse, and satire. He died the year a young woman was born who took the crucial step of introducing science-based speculation as the basis for awe and mystery in her story of *Frankenstein or the Modern Prometheus.*

Mary Godwin (1797–1851), later to become Mary Shelley after marrying Percy Bysshe Shelley, the poet, wrote *Frankenstein* at age 19 as part of a challenge posed by another young, rebellious poet, George Gordon Byron (Lord Byron). He suggested the three of them compete at writing a horror story. Shelley and Byron made some false starts, but never finished the assignment. Mary couldn't even get a good idea at first, but was inspired by a conversation between her husband and Byron regarding some of the work of Dr. Erasmus Darwin (Charles Darwin's grandfather).

Figure 2.3. Mary Shelley created an iconic monster that represented the dangers of irresponsible science.

"Perhaps a corpse would be reanimated," she said; "galvanism had given token of such things: perhaps the component parts of a creature might be manufactured, brought together, and endued with vital warmth" (Panshin, 1989, p. 23).

Mary went to bed after the conversation, but couldn't sleep. She horrified herself with the image of a man using the secrets of chemistry and electricity to raise the dead with powers that mocked "the stupendous mechanism of the Creator of the world." She realized in a burst of insight that what horrified her would horrify others. "I need only describe the spectre which had haunted my midnight pillow." The next day the story flowed from her pen.

The key element in the story that labels it as science fiction is that, although the skills and knowledge of Dr. Frankenstein exceeded any science of the day, it didn't seem *implausible* that those abilities might be achieved in the future. The intelligent reader could sufficiently suspend belief long enough to entertain the possibility that a man could someday "reanimate" lifeless matter, and the reader was also free to ponder seriously the consequences of such ability, free to wonder about a future it might be possible to create—or to avoid.

The century from 1850 to 1950 that followed Shelley's death provided a full measure of wonders, full of sublime achievements, mind-numbing vistas of time and space, as well as horrific tragedies on a monumental scale. *Frankenstein* became synonymous with any product of science out-of-control and monstrous.

Flights and Fantasies

Many of you may remember Edgar Allan Poe (1809–1849) from high school English class. He seems especially perfect for the adolescent male: a tragic genius strung out on alcohol and opium, who is fascinated by lost loves, death, and horror. Even though he wrote in the first third of the nineteenth century and his language seems a bit stilted and florid to modern ears, stories like "The Pit in the Pendulum" and "The Tell-Tale Heart" can still raise a shiver along your spine. "Annabel Lee" can still yank a tear from anyone who has suffered a lost love. Perhaps you never considered Poe an SF writer unless you read titles like "The Unparalleled Adventures of One Hans Pfaall" (1835) (7), which tells about an out-of-work bellows maker who makes a trip to the moon in a balloon. A young Jules Verne, impressed with this story, wrote his own unique variations on some of Poe's scenarios, including "Five Weeks in a Balloon" (1863) and "From the Earth to the Moon" (1865), in which some of his characters refer to Poe as a "strange, moody genius" (Panshin and Panshin, 1989, p. 34).

Although Poe considered his Hans Pfaall story to have great "verisimilitude" with regard to its science content, science content was not an integral element for much of Poe's work. He wrote diligently to create a setting, mood, and tone that would transport the reader out of his or her normal frame of reference. "Poe's stories are all attempts to dislocate perception, using a wide variety of methods" (Panshin and Panshin, 1989, p. 33). Poe, like Mary Shelley, was struggling to reinsert the sense of mystery and possibility into literature for readers who could no longer find it in mythological adventures. As late as the 1920s, some of Poe's work was reprinted in SF pulp magazines, but it was more a tip-of-the-hat to someone who, in retrospect, inspired the SF writers who followed in the next generation.

And the next generation would witness enough scientific wonders to boggle any mind.

NOTES

(1) This inspiring quote may actually have been a half-concealed reference to Hooke's small physical stature. At this point, Hooke and Newton had been squabbling with each other for a decade (see note 6).

(2) 100,000 years is a conservative estimate for fossil remains of *Homo sapiens* fossils. The June 14, 2003, issue of *Science News* reports *H. Sapiens* fossils discovered near Herto, Ethiopia, that are dated between 154,000 and 160,000 years old. Whether these humans had the same faculty for creativity and art demonstrated by the cave paintings of Chauvet cave, perhaps 35,000 years old, is a subject for academic debate.

(3) From *Chambers Biographical Dictionary,* 6th ed., 1997, page 77.

(4) See "Socrates Dies at Delium, 424 B.C." (Hanson, 2001).

(5) Recently, Gavin Menzies has presented convincing evidence that the Chinese may have visited the Americas first in 1421, not to mention circumnavigating the globe. But the Chinese withdrew from world affairs shortly after these voyages, during a period of political and economic instability. See Menzies (2002).

(6) When Newton presented his masterwork the *Principia* to the Royal Society in 1687, Hooke's vanity suffered. He felt that Newton hadn't given him enough credit. "That Newton had given him any credit whatsoever was an act of unaccustomed generosity," says David Berlinski in *Newton's Gift* (2000, p. 94). "Given Hooke's reflexive charge of plagiarism, Newton responded with methodical fury, going over the manuscript of the *Principia* and striking Hooke's name at every turn."

(7) See the *Complete Stories and Poems of Edgar Allan Poe* (Doubleday & Co., 1966).

REFERENCES

Asimov, Isaac. *Asimov's Biographical Encyclopedia of Science and Technology.* New York: Avon Books, 1972.

Berlinski, David. *Newton's Gift.* New York: Free Press, 2000.

Eiseley, Loren. *The Man Who Saw through Time.* New York: Charles Scribner's Sons, 1973.

Hanson, Victor Davis. "Socrates Dies at Delium, 424 B.C." in *What If? 2.* Robert Crowley, ed. New York: G.P. Putnam's Sons, 2001, pp. 1–22.

Kepler, Johannes. "Somnium" (1634). Translated by Edward Rosen in *Kepler's "Somnium,"* 1967.

Menzies, Gavin. *1421: The Year China Discovered America.* New York: William Morrow (HarperCollins), 2002.

Neyman, Jerzy, ed. *The Heritage of Copernicus.* Cambridge, MA: MIT Press, 1974.

Panshin Alexei, and Cory Panshin. *The World beyond the Hill.* Los Angeles: Jeremy P. Tarcher, 1989.

Parry, Melanie, ed. *Chambers Biographical Dictionary,* Centenary Edition. New York: Larousse Kingfisher Chambers, 1997.

Poe, Edgar Allan. "The Unparalleled Adventures of One Hans Pfaall" (1835), in *Complete Stories and Poems of Edgar Allan Poe.* New York: Doubleday & Co., 1966, p. 517.

Shelley, Mary. *Frankenstein or the Modern Prometheus* (1818). New York: Collier, 1961, p. 8.

Suplee, Curto. *Milestones of Science.* Washington, DC: National Geographic, 2000.

ADDITIONAL READING

Bullock, William, M.D., F.R.S. *The History of Bacteriology*. New York: Dover Publications, 1979 (originally published in 1938 by Oxford University Press).

Dobell, Clifford, ed. *Antony Van Leeuwenhoek and His Little Animals*. New York: Dover Publications, 1960 (originally published in 1932 by John Bale, Sons and Danielsson, Ltd.).

Ford, Brian J. *Single Lens—The Story of the Simple Microscope*. New York: Harper & Row, 1985.

Winchester, Simon. *The Map That Changed the World, William Smith and the Birth of Modern Geology*. New York: HarperCollins, 2001.

CHAPTER 3

1850–1950: A Century of Mystery, Awe, and Power

> *"The past is but the beginning of a beginning, and all that is and has been is but the twilight of the dawn . . . "*
>
> H. G. Wells

Copernicus removed humans from the center of the universe and Newton demonstrated that common laws of nature governed both heaven and Earth, but these insights represented only the beginning of rationalism's assault on our collective human ego. The century from 1850 to 1950 would firmly place human beings on a side branch of an evolutionary process that had been grinding away for unimaginable eternities; would reduce even our entire galaxy of stars to one grain of sand among many, and would convert space and time into Einstein's confusing space-time, with very counterintuitive properties. It's no wonder that writers grappled with the consequences of scientific discoveries and, in the process, created the genre of science fiction we recognize today.

Some writers maintained a faith and optimism that human beings could ultimately rise above their lowly origins and prevail against all perils the universe might provide—or at least evolve into entities up to the task. Others looked around them at wars and atrocities magnified by growing technologies and despaired. A centenarian in 1950 had witnessed more changes in her personal lifestyle and her sense of place in the cosmos than any human who had lived before her. In this chapter we'll see how scientific discoveries spawned an imaginative literature that would both revel in a heady sense of awe and power and tremble at dark mysteries and fearful consequences.

DARWIN'S GRAND SYNTHESIS AND DEEP TIME

Man, the Fallen Angel

Charles Darwin (1809–1882), like many a child before him, disappointed his father by not becoming a medical doctor or a reverend—two clearly defined roads to comfort and honor in the nineteenth century. In an effort to "find himself" he accepted a post as naturalist aboard the HMS *Beagle* and sailed away for 5 years to explore the natural history of distant lands. He collected, catalogued, and observed the living things and geological phenomena he witnessed, and ultimately came to an epiphany so threatening to human self-image that it is hotly debated in some quarters today, even though its essential truth is unquestioned by scientists. And even though evolution through natural selection serves as the theoretical underpinning for modern biology, it is perhaps the most misunderstood of scientific discoveries.

Darwin didn't connect all the dots on his own conceptualization until he had read Thomas Malthus' (1766–1834) *An Essay on Population* after he was safely back in England. That publication provided the key concept that populations increase exponentially while food and other

Figure 3.1. Charles Darwin found the unifying principle of biology: change in living creatures over time directed by Nature's selection of the reproductively fit.

resources increase in a linear fashion. Thus, differential reproduction rates caused by differential fitness could explain how populations evolve over time, competing for limited resources. Even with this insight and all the evidence he had collected to back him up, Darwin feared the implications of his own discovery so much that he delayed publication for 20 years. He shared the announcement of his theory with Alfred Russell Wallace (1823–1913), who had reached similar conclusions on parallel voyages of discovery.

Evolution itself was not a concept unique to Darwin. Georges Louis Leclerc de Buffon (1707–1788), the great French naturalist of the previous century, had proposed an evolutionary explanation for the differences he found in plants and animals. Darwin provided a workable mechanism for how evolution could work, limited chiefly by ignorance of the details of inheritance, which must generate the raw materials for natural selection. And although Gregor Mendel's (1822–1884) nearly contemporary work on inheritance in pea plants held the key, it would lie undiscovered for a generation. Mendel would show that inheritance depended on the shuffling of discrete traits passed unchanged, though masked at times, from generation to generation. Others adhered to the theory of Jean-Baptiste Lamarck (1744–1829) that organisms could inherit features that their parents had acquired during their lifetimes. Numbered among these was the French writer who cleverly conceived of the concept of "scientific romances," Jules Verne (1828–1905). Verne wrote only one evolutionary tale (translated as *The Village in the Treetop* in 1964 from his 1901 *La grande foret, le village Aerien*), but it was based on Lamarck's brand of inheritance (Panshin and Panshin, 1989). We'll look at Verne in more detail after discussing one more scientific shocker that was also central to Darwin's arguments for evolution by natural selection: the age of the Earth.

The Abyss of Deep Time

Fossils demonstrate that (1) there were once oceans in places that are now dry land; (2) living things change over time—sometimes quite suddenly; (3) the Earth must have hosted living things for quite some time because sedimentary deposits are so thick (1). The infant science of geology had three theories to explain this state of affairs.

Neptunists claimed that a flood or series of floods periodically scoured the Earth. Catastrophists claimed that a series of disasters wiped out life on Earth after which God created new forms. Plutonists, a minority, argued that the forces of volcanism and erosion could, over time, explain the Earth in its present configuration. James Hutton (1726–1797) supported the latter view in a theory called Uniformitarianism, which proposed that the forces at work today on the Earth are essentially the same as the forces that shaped the world in the past. He believed that the time needed to create the planet we see today was so vast that there was "no vestige of a beginning—no prospect of an end" (2).

Charles Lyell (1797–1875), a lawyer more fascinated with rocks than writs, believed—after extensive observations in France and Italy—that Hutton and the Plutonists had the right idea. Darwin took the first edition of Lyell's book *The Principles of Geology* with him on the *Beagle,* ultimately embracing Uniformitarianism himself. But questions remained: how do you quantify processes, like rates of sedimentation and erosion, that may vary with temperature and weather patterns? For that matter, maybe those rates varied in a radically different past.

A child prodigy named William Thompson (1824–1907) (who later became Baron Kelvin of Largs or Lord Kelvin) decided to help out the mushy-headed geologists by crunching some numbers based on the known laws of physics and chemistry of the day (3). His reasoning was straightforward: If the Earth started out as a molten ball of rock and minerals, one should be able to calculate how long a body of that size would take to cool. With admittedly rough estimates for some factors, he concluded that the Earth couldn't be much older than a hundred million years and could only support life for about twenty-five million years. Scientists still wanted more time. They needed to account for fossil-bearing strata that ultimately totaled 400,000 feet in thickness.

Lord Kelvin's numbers seemed to put the age question to rest until Marie and Pierre Curie (1867–1934, 1859–1906) discovered the elements radium and polonium in pitchblende, an ore of uranium. In addition to producing mysterious "X-rays," these elements also generated a great deal of heat over long periods of time, without being significantly consumed in the process. Since they proved common in the Earth's crust, their existence radically altered Lord Kelvin's age estimates for the planet based on rate of cooling. Also, because radioactive elements decay from one element to another at a constant rate, and because they are not replenished, they provided a potential clock for measuring just how old the Earth is. Ernest Rutherford (1871–1937) led the way in these studies, but it took Arthur Holmes (1890–1965) to champion and refine radioactive dating techniques (Lewis, 2000) that would ultimately peg the Earth's age at something greater than 1.5 billion years by 1931 and 4.6 billion years by today.

This giddy temporal abyss leaves time for many wonders. Darwin would have been pleased if such vistas had become apparent before he published *On the Origin of Species* in 1859. Nevertheless, Lord Kelvin's 25 million years was an enormous number, and the discovery of monstrous fossils of obviously extinct saurians in time for the 1851 Hyde Park Exhibition in London provided a great deal to contemplate for any nineteenth-century visitor, not to mention a particularly visionary one like Jules Verne.

Scientific Romances Evolve . . .

Jules Verne (1828–1905) grew up as Romanticism was fading and science was becoming a respectable occupation and not just a hobby. Applied science assumed the name "technology." In 1851 Verne conceived the idea of writing "science romances" that would be analogous to the historical romances of his literary mentor, Alexandre Dumas (author of *The Three Musketeers* and *The Count of Monte Cristo*). Verne's first published story, "A Balloon Journey," was a metaphor for his generation: A romantic "madman" and a technologist wrestle for control of a balloon. The madman ultimately falls to his death while the technologist finds a way to steer the leaky balloon safely back to Earth (Panshin and Panshin, 1989).

The following quote from *The United States Review* of 1853 gives an idea of the confidence science inspired at the time: "Within half a century, machinery will perform all work—automata will direct them. The only tasks of the human race will be to make love, study, and be happy" (Ochoa and Corey, 1995). Ah, well. Just a little premature.

Verne's scientific romances caught on. Ultimately, he fulfilled every writer's wish: to make a living from practicing his craft. Verne wrote 65 books of "voyages extraordinaire," but most of us growing up in the twentieth century remember two above all: *Journey to the Center of the Earth* (1864) and *20,000 Leagues under the Sea* (1869–70).

Journey to the Center of the Earth may represent his most imaginative voyage. In it his characters explore one of the last uncharted regions of the planet at the time and find a legendary volcano in the wilds of Iceland that leads to a hidden world beneath the Earth. Here his narrator, Axel, who is the romantic man of mystery, witnesses a vision that takes him the length and breadth of Earth's long history.

In *20,000 Leagues under the Sea* Verne created his most memorable piece of technology, the submarine *Nautilus,* powered by some clever manipulation of "electrical forces" by Captain Nemo. But just as Nemo charges his submarine into the turbulent waters of a submarine abyss, the narrator gets knocked unconscious and awakes at a fisherman's cottage in the Lofoten Islands. Verne takes the reader on more substantial journeys than Poe was capable of, but he pulls back at the edge and tantalizes with a glimpse of unrealized mysteries (Panshin and Panshin, 1989). Verne stands as a true pioneer of the genre, but an Englishman named Herbert George Wells (1866–1946) took his readers to the brink of wonder and beyond.

. . . Into Science Fiction

Wells studied biology under the tutelage of Thomas Henry Huxley (1825–1895) (4), sometimes referred to as Darwin's Bulldog for his aggressive support of Darwin's theory of natural selection. Huxley's successful 1860 debate with Bishop Samuel Wilberforce (1805–1873) contributed to that image. It's not surprising that Wells absorbed the Darwinian slant on evolution's mechanisms, which included catchphrases like "survival of the fittest" and "red in tooth and claw." Wells worried that the same qualities that allowed *Homo sapiens* to survive and endure might preclude the development of a truly just society (Clute and Nicholls, 1993). Works like *The Time Machine* (1895), *The Island of Dr. Moreau* (1896), *The War of the Worlds* (1898), and *The Croquet Player* (1936) all reflected those concerns. In *The Time Machine,* the time traveler speculates that the Morlocks may once have been servants of the Eloi, but they each evolved their separate ways. "The Eloi, like the Carlovingian Kings, had decayed to a mere beautiful futility. They still possessed the earth on sufferance: since the Morlocks, subterranean for innumerable generations, had come at last to find the daylit surface intolerable" (Chapter VII).

Unlike Verne, Wells was not afraid to fully enter realms of scientific mystery. "I drew a breath, set my teeth, and went off with a thud. The night came, like the turning off of a lamp, and in another moment came tomorrow" (Chapter III), says his time traveler. And the reader soon emerges into the world of A.D. 802,701 to confront the delicate grace of the Eloi. Perhaps the difference was that Wells grew up with some of the practical, technological fruits of science—including the negative ones of weapons technology first displayed in the Franco-Prussian War of 1870–71.

Wells confronted the expanding wonder and mystery of the universe and scared people with

Figure 3.2. H. G. Wells learned humility from the discoveries of science, but also maintained a certain optimism: "A day will come," he said, "when beings who are now latent in our thoughts and hidden in our loins shall stand upon this earth as one stands on a footstool, and shall laugh and reach out their hands amid the stars."

it. A generation later, Orson Welles succeeded in scaring an even wider audience in Depression-era America with his radio broadcast version of *The War of the Worlds*. Wells' doubts about human competence in a vast and frightening universe is reflected in the powerful ending: the Martians fall, not to anything human beings can assault them with, but to Earth viruses against which they have no defenses.

Wells promoted his visions quite effectively in nonfiction and journalistic essays as well. His *Outline of History* (1920) sold two million copies and held a spot on the best-seller list for four years running. And you can blame his famous essay entitled "The Man of the Year Million" for the popular image of the short, physically weak, but bulbous-headed, big-eyed genius that *Homo sapiens* might evolve into. (This future vision of humanity also bears a striking resemblance to the popular description of UFO aliens.)

AN EXPANDING UNIVERSE AND DISTORTED SPACE-TIME

The Abyss of Deep Space

As time stretched to barely conceivable near-infinities, space expanded to mind-bending distances. Henrietta Leavitt (1868–1921) discovered a type of star whose energy output varied in a regular way. These Cepheid variable stars had stronger outputs when they had longer cycles and weaker outputs with short cycles. The distance to nearby Cepheids could be measured by triangulation. The distance to far-away Cepheids could be inferred from their apparent brightness, which declines with distance in a regular way. Harlow Shapley (1885–1972) used Cepheid yardsticks to measure the size of our Milky Way and our sun's place in it. Edwin Hubble (1889–1953) used Cepheid variable stars to show that distant "gas clouds" were really other galaxies, and that they were speeding away from our own galaxy as if they were part of an ancient explosion (the so-called Big Bang). In 1964, Bell Lab scientists discovered the background hiss of radiation that marked this primal event (Suplee, 2000).

The Linkage of Space and Time

Albert Einstein (1879–1955), a patent office clerk with a flair for mathematics, demonstrated in 1905 that distance and time were not the absolutes that common sense dictates. He showed that at velocities approaching the speed of light, time and distance vary depending on the observer. Following this Special Theory of Relativity, Einstein proposed a General Theory of Relativity that made gravity the result of mass bending the fabric of the newly created space-time. The theory predicted that our sun's mass should bend light passing near it, which was confirmed by Arthur Eddington (1882–1944) during an eclipse in 1919. The theory also led to Einstein's famous equation, $E = mc^2$, which demonstrates that mass and energy are interchangeable. Einstein, like Newton, achieved a fame during his own lifetime of nearly "pop star" proportions.

Figure 3.3. Albert Einstein, like Newton, transformed human perceptions of how the universe operated and quantified nature's laws in ways that unleashed awesome and frightening powers.

Underlying Unities

The universe, through the lens of scientific scrutiny, grew vaster, older, and stranger during this hundred-year period, but old and new observations were also falling into patterns that gave scientists the ability to make powerful predictions and to tap sobering energies. Dimitry Mendeleyev (1834–1907) arranged the 60 known elements of his day in a table based on their atomic weights and chemical properties. The table led to predictions (soon fulfilled) of future elements and what their basic physical/chemical properties should be. This Periodic Table of the Elements showed that chemical properties depended on atomic structure and gave chemists a powerful tool to organize their science.

Josef von Fraunhofer (1787–1826) showed that every element has its own unique light spectrum. Together with two other scientists, von Fraunhofer developed the spectroscope. With this tool, scientists were able to "read" the composition of distant suns by scanning the light spectra they produced. James Clerk Maxwell (1831–1879) showed that not only were electricity and magnetism variations of the same thing—forms of electromagnetic radiation—but that light and other forms of energy were part of this continuum as well (Suplee, 2000).

Einstein's mass/energy equivalency, of course, led to the conversion of a small amount of mass into a vast amount of energy in the form of an atomic bomb. The energy of a thermonuclear explosion could be, and was, used to fuse hydrogen into helium in the hydrogen bomb—the same process that occurs in the sun.

SCIENCE, TECHNOLOGY, AND HUMAN AFFAIRS

Science Fiction and the First "Rocket Scientist"

Every October 19, Robert H. Goddard (1882–1945) celebrated "Anniversary Day." On that day in 1899 when he was 17, he saw a vision of a rocket thundering into the sky toward the moon. He kept that vision clearly in mind while pursuing graduate degrees at Clark University, working as a research fellow at Princeton, suffering experimental failures, scrounging for money, and enduring ridicule in the press for being an "impractical dreamer" (Haven and Clark, 1999). He persevered to invent the first multistage rocket and patented 213 other ideas that became the basis of modern rocketry. In 1920, the *New York Times* published an editorial that ridiculed Goddard's concept that rockets could escape Earth's gravity and reach the moon. By 1937, Goddard had built rockets that attained heights of 9,000 feet; but after his attempts to create jet engines for aircraft failed, he lost military funding for his work. Nearly 25 years after his death in 1945, the *Times* printed a retraction of their earlier editorial when Neil Armstrong stepped onto the surface of the moon.

While science can inspire imaginative literature, Goddard showed that imaginative literature can spark a vision that may advance science and directly influence the future. One of the sources for his early dreams of spaceflight came from reading Wells' *War of the Worlds* (Haven and Clark, 1999).

Goddard's counterpart in Russia, Konstantin Tsiolkovsky (1857–1935), provided the Soviet Union with the technology to launch their *Sputnik* satellites in 1957, shocking a complacent United States. The United States would have been further behind without the acquired expertise of the defeated Germans.

Werner Von Braun (1912–1977) desperately wanted space travel to happen, but he grew up in Germany to face the realities of World War II, where the German military saw rockets as vehicles for bombs. He agreed to work for the German Ordnance Department if they paid for his college education, which they did. In 1937 he became the civilian head of the Peenemuende Rocket Center and built the Vengeance Weapon 2 (V-2) rockets that were used to bomb London. In

1945, he delivered his entire research team to the U.S. Army with the agreement that they be allowed to continue making rockets for space travel. He ultimately *became* the U.S. space program, designing rockets that served U.S. military and civilian agencies for 30 years, and was instrumental in the formation of NASA, the National Aeronautics and Space Administration. He built the Saturn vehicles that carried out John F. Kennedy's mission to place a man on the moon by the end of the sixties.

War-Born Dystopias and Other Dark Visions

After the devastating loss of life during World War I, science seemed to be a tool of destruction that men were bound to abuse. Aldous Huxley's *Brave New World* (1932) and James Hilton's *Lost Horizon* (1932) portrayed Earth-based dystopias built on human ambition and misuse of technology. In Karel Capek's *War with the Newts* (1937), human beings exploit a newly-found intelligent race of amphibians—until these newts learn to emulate us well enough to do their own exploiting. H. G. Wells was perhaps the first to speculate in print on using the energy of the atom discovered by Marie and Pierre Curie as a bomb in *The World Set Free* (1914). He describes a world devastated by an atomic holocaust, which rises—phoenix-like—from its own ashes.

This excerpt from Wells' *War of the Worlds* pretty well summarizes his philosophy: "With infinite complacency men went to and fro over this little globe about their affairs, dreaming themselves the highest creatures in the whole vast universe, and serene in their assurance of their empire over matter. It is just possible that the infusoria under the microscope do the same."

For me, one writer or most eloquently summarized speculations on human evolution, destiny, and place in the universe based on scientific knowledge during this century: Olaf Stapledon (1886–1950). One book, *Star Maker* (1937), sketched out SF themes that would be elaborated on by subsequent writers for two generations. He wrote his first novel, *Last and First Men,* in 1930, after much of the science under discussion had been established. The "war to end all wars" concluded, but the groundwork for another was in place, which may explain his somewhat somber outlook.

Last and First Men ranges over the next 2 billion years and 18 races of human beings. The story is told from the viewpoint of an individual of the eighteenth race working through the "docile but scarcely adequate brain" of one of the first men (ourselves). The reader shares the expansion of humankind throughout the solar system, but the last men, looking outward to distant suns, have lost their energy and resolve. They are sure that interstellar voyages would drive human minds to insanity.

The Optimism of America's Golden Age of "Scientifiction"

The United States came out on the winning side of two world wars and inherited some of the best scientific minds of Germany after the second of them. World War II also jump-started America's economy after the doldrums of the Depression. Perhaps its not surprising that an individual arose—Hugo Gernsback—who saw the promises and positive potentials of science and technology and found a way to appeal to a mass audience—especially young males of an academic bent yearning for strange and exotic adventures.

Gernsbach's *Amazing Stories* magazine became science fiction's flagship publication in 1926. He coined the term "scientifiction" for the kind of stories he published and described them this way: "If we may voice our opinion we should say that the ideal proportion of a scientifiction story should be 75% literature interwoven with 25% science" (Panshin and Panshin, 1989, p. 170). E. E. (Doc) Smith (1890–1965) became a popular writer for the magazine and developed a swashbuckling style that has become known as "Space Opera." Brian Aldiss, a British SF author, said: "Beneath Smith's advance, the light years went down like 9-pins and the sober facts of science were appropriated for a binge of impossible adventures. Smith set the Injuns among the stars . . ." (Scholes and Rabkin, 1977, p. 38).

In the thirties, a young writer, John W. Campbell, wanted to create a "new" kind of science fiction that would incorporate more realistic characters and be truer to the underlying science. In 1938 he became editor of *Astounding* and proceeded to nourish and develop writers that he felt were up to the task. His efforts over the next decade or so produced such a crop of impressive writers that the period is often called the "Golden Age" of science fiction, although it really only refers to American-generated work. Four writers stand out: Robert Heinlein (1907–1988), Isaac Asimov (1920–1992), A. E. Van Vogt (1912–2000), and Theodore Sturgeon (1918–1985). In addition to being quality writers, each approached the genre in unique ways that would serve as templates for future practitioners of the craft.

Robert Heinlein: Soldier to the Stars

Heinlein, a former naval officer and student of physics, served as the nucleus of Campbell's core writers and remained one of the most important writers in the SF genre for much of the twentieth century. He wrote quickly, with confidence, and his characters interacted in future worlds whose history, politics, and religions seemed natural and well conceived. He constructed a future history timeline to which each of his stories in *Astounding* could be pegged. Readers read to discover and live in his future full of technological marvels, in the body of savvy protagonists who knew how to get things done.

Many of these stories are collected in *The Man Who Sold the Moon* (1950), *The Green Hills of Earth* (1951), and *Revolt in 2100* (1953). One of his short stories from 1942, "Waldo," gave rise to the term used to describe robots slaved to human motions (see "References" in Chapter 6). "Common Sense" (1941) introduces the concept of generation starships (where several generations are born and die en route to other star systems). One of his early novels, *Methuselah's Children* (1941), introduces Lazarus Jones, a member of a clan of near-immortals whose life ranges over much of Heinlein's future history.

Heinlein never abused science when telling his stories. This is one reason his titles for young readers make such good teacher resources in physics. *Rocket Ship Galileo* (1947) became the basis for an important SF movie in 1950: *Destination Moon* (see Chapter 4). Other excellent early-Heinlein juveniles include *Space Cadet* (1948), *Starman Jones* (1953), and *The Star Beast* (1954). Heinlein also sold to the *Saturday Evening Post* and other mainstream publications of merit, which gave him out-of-genre respectability as well. Heinlein, an optimist when it came to human ingenuity, became more pessimistic as he grew older about human political and religious institutions that hampered individual freedom.

Isaac Asimov: Robots and Galactic Empires

Asimov, another writer whose influence spans much of the twentieth century, has been accused of sacrificing character to the exploration of "neat" ideas. Few other writers could get away with so much character dialogue (as opposed to action) to advance their stories. But the fact is, Asimov stories work—and work well. One story, "Nightfall" (1941), has consistently been voted the "best science fiction story of all time" by members of SFWA (Science Fiction and Fantasy Writers of America), although Asimov himself disagreed in his autobiography (5). "Nightfall" tells the story of a man alive on a planet that follows a complex orbit around multiple suns such that there is complete darkness only once every 2,000 years. At that time, its inhabitants see the stars—and, with echoes of Stapledon's theme in *Last and First Men,* it drives them mad. "Thirty thousand mighty suns shone down in a soul-searing splendor that was more frighteningly cold in its awful indifference than the bitter wind that shivered across the cold, horribly bleak world."

One of his very next projects, *Foundation* (1942), eventually became part of a novel trilogy that the Science Fiction Book Club recently voted the second most important SF/Fantasy title of the last 50 years (beaten out only by Tolkien's *The Lord of the Rings*) (6). The story tells of a galactic human empire that a scientist (a "psychohistorian" named Hari Seldon) believes is on the verge of collapse. He proposes a plan to reduce the resultant period of barbarism to a mere thousand years that involves creating a Foundation of scientists to implement it. Complications arise when a future leader—a mutant of unexpected talents—threatens to derail Seldon's course of action. The third novel introduces a secret, Second Foundation that operates on somewhat different principles. Asimov, a student of history, drew on Gibbon's *The Rise and Fall of the Roman Empire* for inspiration.

"Strange Playfellow" (1940) introduced Robbie the Robot, the first of Asimov's many robot stories and novels. "Liar" (1941) introduced his classic three laws of robotics (see Chapter 8, "Artificial Life on Trial"). His early robot stories are collected in *I, Robot* (1950). Asimov would spend much of the next fifty years expanding on themes generated during this prolific early period and ultimately weaving a common future history that tied together his robot and Foundation futures.

Figure 3.4. Isaac Asimov wrote over 200 books of fact and fiction during his life and gave us templates for galactic empires and robotic behavior.

Van Vogt and "Hard SF Dreams"

Canadian-born A. E. Van Vogt first published in *Astounding Science Fiction* in 1939 with a story called "Black Destroyer." He specialized in intricately plotted, somewhat metaphysical "space opera" tales that one critic described as "hard SF dreams." He wrote organically and sometimes relied on his own dreams to get out of plot predicaments. Looked at critically, many of his stories are rambling and internally inconsistent, but as in a dream, a young, rapt reader will suspend disbelief and go along for the ride.

Like Stapledon's and Asimov's, many of Van Vogt's stories ranged over broad temporal canvasses, as evident from one of his titles: *Two Hundred Million A.D.* (1964). He created nearly invincible monsters, played with time paradox plot elements, and liked "supermen-style" characters like Jommy Cross in his most famous book, *Slan* (1946). Jommy, like other "strange" children, is persecuted by the Hitleresque political powers of his day. Jommy's mother dies in the opening scene and he spends the rest of the book trying to connect with others of his kind (the Slan). He ultimately confronts the dictator who has been his archenemy only to discover—in one of Van Vogt's improbable plot twists—that he is Slan, too.

Other well-known titles include *The Weapon Shops of Isher* (1941–42), *The World of Null-A* (1945), and *The Voyage of the Space Beagle* (serialized in *ASF* from 1939 to 1943).

Theodore Sturgeon: The Writer's Writer

Theodore Sturgeon also wrote of supermen. "Baby Is Three" appeared in *Galaxy* in 1952, telling the story of an assortment of misfit children with strange powers who, together, were much more than any of them individually. This story, merged with two later novellas, became his best-known book, *More than Human* (1953). Many of his story themes (and he wrote approximately 175 short stories) dealt with alienated individuals—often children—who find some sort of transcendent community. He is considered one of the best SF literary stylists. He wrote prolifically when he wrote, but his career suffered several fallow periods when he traveled and did other things. If you read nothing else of his, check out *More than Human*.

In fact, if you become interested in the "superman" or "evolved man" theme, a great sequence of books to explore and contrast would be the following (in chronological order): *The Food of the Gods* by H. G. Wells, *Odd John* by Olaf Stapledon, *Slan* by A. E. Van Vogt, *More than Human* by Theodore Sturgeon, and *Childhood's End* by Arthur C. Clarke.

Wrestling with Immensities

Scientific discoveries, during the latter half of the nineteenth and first half of the twentieth centuries, displaced human beings from any special place in time and space and suggested that God, if He or She existed, might be more of an impersonal innovator rather than a father figure. Fiction writers picked up on these powerful themes and created an imaginative literature that not only tried to make sense of these discoveries, but imbued an emotional energy that provided, in various measures, comfort, resignation, hope, and excitement. Some writers showed how we can derive a certain comfort from understanding how the universe works and our role in its grand and complex interactions. Others resigned us to uncertainty about the specifics of the future and our impermanence, not only as individuals, but as a species. The optimists held out hope for greater understanding and control of nature and reveled in the excitement of worlds yet unvisited and adventures still to come.

But science and the literature of science fiction was just getting started. The next 50 years, as we shall see, provides a wealth of discoveries to contemplate and a cadre of writers to spin out their implications with increased skill and finesse.

NOTES

(1) Simon Winchester tells the engaging story of William Smith (1769–1839), an English surveyor who was nearly cheated out of the fruits of his life's work by members of the fledgling Geological Society who felt somehow justified in purloining the work of a mere commoner. Smith, working in mines and surveying for canal construction, realized that rock layers and the fossils they contained were distinct and recognizable over large areas of England and could provide a measure of relative ages. Smith's geological map of England, 20 years in the making, "changed the world," as the book's title implies.

(2) Several good books deal with the development of the geological time scale. My favorites are *The Abyss of Time* by Claude C. Albritton, Jr., and *The Dating Game* by Cherry Lewis. The former outlines the historical development of changes in determining the age of the Earth and the latter deals with the contributions of Arthur Holmes to the development of radiometric dating techniques.

(3) A good treatment of Lord Kelvin's contribution is given in *Lord Kelvin and the Age of the Earth* by Joe D. Burchfield.

(4) Aldous Huxley (1894–1963), author of *Brave New World* (1932), was the grandson of T. H. Huxley.

(5) Asimov believed his best story (and maybe the best SF story anyone ever wrote, in Asimov's "secret—but not humble—opinion") was "The Last Question," written in 1956.

(6) Reported in *USA Today,* Tuesday, March 4, 2003. Their top ten were: (1) *Lord of the Rings* (Tolkien), 1953–54, (2) *The Foundation Trilogy* (Asimov), 1963, (3) *Dune* (Herbert), 1965, (4) *Stranger in a Strange Land* (Heinlein), 1961, (5) *Wizard of Earthsea* (LeGuin), 1968, (6) *Neuromancer* (Gibson), 1984, (7) *Childhood's End* (Clarke), 1953, (8) *Do Androids Dream of Electric Sheep?* (Dick), 1968, (9) *The Mists of Avalon* (Bradley), 1983, and (10) *Fahrenheit 451* (Bradbury), 1953.

REFERENCES

Albritton, Clark C. Jr. *The Abyss of Time*. Los Angeles: Jeremy P. Tarcher, 1986.

Asimov, Isaac. *The Foundation Trilogy*. New York: Doubleday & Co., 1963.

Asimov, Isaac. *Nightfall and Other Stories*. New York: Doubleday, 1969, p. 2.

Asimov, Isaac. "Strange Playfellow" (1940) appears as "Robbie" in *I, Robot*. New York: Doubleday & Co., 1950, p. 9. "Liar" (1941) appears in *I, Robot*, p. 82.

Burchfield, Joe D. *Lord Kelvin and the Age of the Earth*. Chicago and London: University of Chicago Press, 1990.

Capek, Karel. *War with the Newts* (1937). New York: Berkley Medallion Books, 1965.

Clarke, Arthur C. *Childhood's End*. New York: Ballantine Books, 1953.

Clute, John, and Peter Nicholls. *The Encyclopedia of Science Fiction*. New York: St. Martin's Griffin, 1993 (update 1995).

Desmond, Adrian, and James Moore. *Darwin—The Life of a Tormented Evolutionist*. New York: Time Warner Books, 1991.

Haven, Kendall, and Donna Clark. *100 Most Popular Scientists for Young Adults*. Englewood, CO: Libraries Unlimited, 1999.

Heinlein, Robert A. "Common Sense" (1941) in *Orphans of the Sky*. New York: Berkley Books, 1970, c. 1963.

Heinlein, Robert A. *The Past through Tomorrow*. New York: G.P. Putnam's Sons, 1967. "The Man Who Sold the Moon," p. 98; "The Green Hills of Earth," p. 294; "Methuselah's Children," p. 526.

Heinlein, Robert A. *Revolt in 2100*. New York: Signet Books, 1953.

Heinlein, Robert A. *Rocket Ship Galileo*. New York: Scribner, 1947.

Heinlein, Robert A. *Space Cadet*. New York: Ace, 1948.

Heinlein, Robert A. *The Star Beast*. New York: Ace Books, 1954.

Heinlein, Robert A. *Starman Jones*. New York: Scribner, 1953.

Heinlein, Robert A. "Waldo" in *Waldo and Magic, Inc.* Boston: Gregg Press, 1979, p. 13.

Hilton, James. *Lost Horizon* (1932). New York: W. Morrow, 1936.

Huxley, Aldous. *Brave New World* (1932). New York: Harper & Row, 1969.

Lewis, Cherry. *The Dating Game—One Man's Search for the Age of the Earth*. London: Cambridge University Press, 2000.

Ochoa, George, and Melinda Corey. *The Timeline Book of Science*. New York: Ballantine Books, 1995.

Panshin, Alexei, and Cory Panshin. *The World beyond the Hill*. Los Angeles: Jeremy P. Tarcher, 1989.

Scholes, Robert, and Eric S. Rabkin. *Science Fiction: History, Science, Vision*. New York: Oxford University Press, 1977.

Stapledon, Olaf. *Last and First Men* (1930). Baltimore, MD: Penguin Books, 1973.

Stapledon, Olaf. *Odd John* (1935). New York: A Berkley Medallion Book, 1965.

Sturgeon, Theodore. "Baby Is Three" (1952 in *Galaxy Magazine*) is the first part of *More than Human* (1953). New York: Ballantine Books, 1960.

Suplee, Curt. *Milestones of Science*. Washington, DC: National Geographic, 2000.

Van Vogt, A. E. *Slan*. New York: Ballantine Books, 1961.

Van Vogt, A. E. *Two Hundred Million A.D.* New York: Paperback Library, 1964.

Van Vogt, A. E. *The Weapon Shops of Isher*. New York: Ace Publishing Corp., 1951.

Van Vogt, A. E. *The Voyage of the Space Beagle* (1939–43). New York: Pocket Books, 1977.

Van Vogt, A. E. *The World of Null-A* (1945). New York: Berkeley, 1970.

Verne, Jules. *Journey to the Center of the Earth* (1864). New York: Penguin, 1965.

Verne, Jules. *20,000 Leagues under the Sea* (1869–70). New York: Random House, 1983.

Wells, H. G. *The Croquet Player* (1936). New York: Viking Press, 1937.

Wells, H. G. *The Food of the Gods*. New York: Ballantine Books, n.d.

Wells, H. G. *The Island of Dr. Moreau* (1896) and *The War of the Worlds* (1898) appear in *Seven Famous Novels*. New York: Knopf, 1934.

Wells, H. G. *The Last War: A World Set Free* (1914). Lincoln, NE, and London: University of Nebraska Press, 2001.

Wells, H. G. *The Time Machine* (1895). New York: Berkley Publishing Corp., 1957.

ADDITIONAL READING

Wells, H. G. *The Outline of History*. New York: Doubleday & Co., 1949.

Winchester, Simon. *The Map That Changed the World, William Smith and the Birth of Modern Geology*. New York: HarperCollins, 2001.

CHAPTER 4

1950–2000: A Half-Century of Space Travel, Computers, and Biorevolutions

"I render infinite thanks to God for being so kind as to make me alone the first observer of marvels kept hidden in obscurity for all previous centuries."

Galileo Galilei

Science has provided us with fundamental principles that describe how the universe operates. Practical-minded people have converted this understanding to technologies that allow us to live longer, more comfortable lives. The trade-offs have included living faster, more frenetic existences, at least in the industrialized world, contending with human populations exceeding 6 billion—with all the problems of pollution, conflict, and ecological collapse that follow in its wake, and coping with constant change in what we do and how we do it. The literature of science fiction, as it did in the previous hundred years, mirrors these discoveries and social changes, including significantly more female voices in the mix.

Science began by studying phenomena of force and power and cataloging the living world. In the second half of the twentieth century, scientists sought to unify physical laws into a "Theory of Everything." The life sciences matured, beginning with the discovery of the genetic code in 1954. Fieldwork revealed ecological patterns in modern communities and built a framework around the organizing principle of evolution that provided great insights into the origin and long development of life on Earth. Chemists began understanding enough about atomic and molecular behavior that they could effectively design unique materials like plastics and delve into the biochemistries of living systems. The fruits of fundamental mathematics found their way into the search for the truly interactive machine and artificial intelligence, as well as the broad application of things like fractals and chaos theory.

Technological spin-offs from science swept us away to deal with TV, radio, desktop computers, space probes, robots, genetic engineering, the Internet, disease therapies, cell phones, and a host of other things. In science fiction, the quality of writing improved considerably. Some authors picked up old themes and many times handled them with more finesse. But social changes and environmental concerns came to the fore, as well. Women, liberated from large families and traditional roles, put words to their concerns and experiences. A "New Wave" of science fiction took a literary and critical look at the state of the world as wrought by science. Computers and virtual reality spawned a brand of SF called "Cyberpunk." But let's begin with a "core" topic of SF speculation: the allure of space travel.

EXPLORING THE BOUNDLESS FRONTIER

The Realities of Space Flight and Maturing Physical Sciences

The team of engineers and technicians assembled by von Braun and NASA during the 1950s and 1960s accomplished miracles to send men to the moon and back with the equivalent of a Commodore 64 computer. Anything seemed possible. But politics provided darker visions. President Kennedy urged families to build or buy bomb shelters (which most couldn't afford), and I can remember marching to our school's shelter and lining up next to the boxes of canned goods and crackers to practice emergency procedures. When the United States blockaded Russian missile shipments to Cuba, I wondered if we would see a mushroom cloud on the horizon—and if anything could survive such an event.

But the Cuban Missile Crisis passed. Tensions lessened. After Neil Armstrong stepped on moon dust and took his "giant leap for mankind" on July 20, 1969, I looked forward to seeing space stations and planetary explorations within my lifetime. Perhaps I would step on another world someday, if not as an explorer, at least as a tourist. But by then Kennedy was dead and war in Vietnam eroded public spirit and drained public funds.

Space exploration didn't end in the seventies, but much of it was conducted by remote control. *Pioneers 10* and *11*, launched in 1972 and 1973, respectively, photographed Jupiter and Saturn in exciting detail. *Pioneer 10* went on to become the first "escapee" from the solar system in 1986 and didn't fall silent until January 31, 2003—82 times as far from Earth as the sun. *Viking I* landed on Mars in July of 1976. Unfortunately, *Viking*'s tests proved inconclusive and Mars stills hides definitive evidence of present or past life forms, despite recent claims of possible fossil microbes in ancient meteorites believed to have a Martian origin. *Pioneers 12* and *13* explored Venus in 1978, revealing how inhospitable a planet with a runaway "greenhouse" atmosphere can be. Two *Voyager* spacecraft launched in 1977 explored Jupiter and Saturn again with cameras and instrumentation and left the solar system with a plaque and sound recordings proclaiming our existence and home planet—a "Kilroy was here" message to any spacefaring intelligences that might be at large (Ochoa and Corey, 1995).

Unmanned space explorations continued in the eighties with Russian and American probes to Venus. The American space shuttle program began with the launch of *Columbia* in 1981. Three others followed, but the program became delayed when *Challenger* exploded in 1986 and when *Columbia* disintegrated on re-entry in 2003. Both events, filmed and rebroadcast many times, demonstrated in real and immediate terms the costs of exploration. *Discovery* launched in 1988 and in 1989 deployed the first space probe from orbit. The Russians orbited two space stations during the eighties, *Salyut 7* and *Mir*, and her astronauts set endurance records. In 1989 astronomers made two discoveries on a grander scale: Enormous black holes apparently anchor the center of galaxies—at least they do in the Andromeda and M32 galaxies in our local cluster of galaxies—and a "great wall" of galaxies forms the largest known "structure" in the universe (Ochoa and Corey, 1995).

Black holes—the remains of giant stars that have collapsed to near-infinite densities, so that space is severely "bent" and time ends—were mathematically described by Steven Hawking (1942–) and Roger Penrose (1931–) in the mid-sixties. They became co-proposers of the concept that the "Big Bang" that started the expansion of the universe was a massive black hole or singularity. Hawking, the heir of Newton and Einstein—and the victim of a crippling neuromotor disease—gained popularity with his 1988 book *A Brief History of Time*. Hawking also pursues Einstein's goal of creating a Grand Unification Theory (GUT)—a "Theory of Everything"—that will unite general relativity, thermodynamics, and quantum mechanics. Such a theory, he says, would be "the ultimate triumph of human reason, for then we would surely know the mind of God" (Haven and Clark, 1999).

The 1990s saw the launch of the Hubble Space Telescope, which has provided breathtaking views of the distant heavens—after having its bad lens exchanged during a shuttle visit. More unmanned flights continued. *Galileo* photographed an asteroid and revisited Jupiter. Paying attention to asteroids gained importance after 1992 when the impact site of a wayward asteroid that may have ended the dinosaurs' tenure on Earth 65 million years ago was discovered in the Yucatan peninsula of Mexico (1). *Magellan* mapped Venus with radar. *Ulysses* studied the poles of the sun. Scientists achieved controlled nuclear fusion reactions, but they are still not practical for power plants. The long-sought elementary particle called a "Top Quark" was found and the core of the International Space Station now circles in orbit. Japan, the United States, and the European Space Agency launched a total of six spacecraft in the late 1990s that are, as of early 2004, either en route to, orbiting, or sitting on the surface of Mars. The U.S. rovers, *Spirit* and *Opportunity,* combined with the orbiters, *Global Surveyor* and *Odyssey,* seek to learn more about the role of water of Mars, both in carving the features of the red planet and as a facilitator for any Martian life—past or present.

The New Realities of Planetary Exploration

The realities of space probe surveys of the solar system removed the scientific underpinnings of some of the romantic speculations in which SF authors had engaged in the first part of the twentieth century. Mars provides some of the clearest examples. When the Italian astronomer Giovanni Schiaparelli (1835–1910) described *canali* (channels) on the surface of Mars and the American astronomer Percival Lowell (1855–1916) interpreted them as possible evidence of a Martian civilization, SF authors like Edgar Rice Burroughs were free to populate Mars with strange kingdoms and weave fantastic adventures. Even as late as 1950, Ray Bradbury created a seductive collection of stories, *The Martian Chronicles,* that involved various Earth explorers of the red planet haunted by the ghosts of Martians past as well as their own personal demons. Without hard evidence to the contrary until the *Viking* landing of 1976, Mars held hopes of being at least a former abode of life—even of the civilized sort.

Mars failed or left ambiguous *Viking*'s tests for life and showed it to be crater-pocked, cold, and nearly airless—though with some evidence that water had at one time created some of its features. Writers of "hard" (scientifically grounded) SF applied themselves to finding practical ways to reach, explore, and perhaps colonize this neighbor planet. Some early works that took this approach (even though they were pre-*Viking*) include *Sands of Mars* (1951) by Arthur C. Clarke, *Red Planet* (1949), a juvenile by Robert Heinlein, and *Welcome to Mars* (1967) by James Blish. Theodore Sturgeon, the "literary" part of Campbell's Golden Age quartet, wrote a poignant short tale about a dying astronaut in "The Man Who Lost the Sea" (1959). Ben Bova, writer and editor of both science fact and science fiction, continued in the tradition of Clarke and others with the novel *Mars* (1992). Refer also to the Mars novels of Kim Stanley Robinson and Robert Heinlein's pop classic, *Stranger in a Strange Land* (which has a "classic" Martian plot element), mentioned later in this chapter.

But, by the sixties, many young SF writers felt that traditional science fiction was becoming too formulaic and resistant to new styles and subjects. They became sensitive to criticisms that SF was not really "literature."

New Wave SF

John W. Campbell gave science fiction a credo: astonish the reader with scientifically plausible ideas and demonstrate how wondrous the future may be. He encouraged writers to write well, but to write directly and simply, in the service of a great idea. The writing style shouldn't be clever or elegant for its own sake to the point where it commands the majority of the reader's

Figure 4.1. Mars entices human imagination with the possibility of life—past or present.

attention. SF readers, for the most part, tend to support Campbell's assertions. As David Hartwell says in *Age of Wonders* (1984), "they are the children of H. G. Wells, not Henry James."

When Campbell passed from the scene, a "New Wave" science fiction arose that not only stressed literary style, but tended to render the roles of science and technology in more somber, pessimistic tones. Author J. G. Ballard defined New Wave science fiction with a series of "disaster novels," including *The Wind from Nowhere* (1962) and *The Drowned World* (1962). Judith Merrill and Michael Moorcock (editor of a British magazine called *New Worlds*) became Ballard's biggest advocates. Moorcock's magazine published and encouraged SF writers who emphasized character and literary style. Others in the field claimed Ballard's work to be "anti-SF," largely because of its pessimistic tone and preoccupation with the "softer" sciences of psychology that dealt more with "inner space." In 1971, John J. Pierce declared: "In 'New Wave' fiction, science *always* leads only to disastrous results, humanity is *always* presented as evil, helpless and insignificant; the universe is *always* a nightmare beyond rational comprehension; and the philosophy is *always* nihilistic or deterministic" (Hartwell, 1984, p. 148).

To be fair, writers categorized as part of the New Wave, like Harlan Ellison, Robert Silverberg, Roger Zelazny, and John Brunner, did improve the quality of the literature of science fiction. The fact that various counterculture elements, like mind-altering drugs, Eastern religions, sex, breaking of taboos, and political cynicism, crept into the mix may have exacerbated the friction with more conservative writers. The stories in Harlan Ellison's *Dangerous Visions* (1967) don't seem particularly radical by today's standards, but they moved beyond Campbell's vision. Isaac Asimov, who wrote the introduction for Ellison, praised the stories within as being part of the "Second Revolution" in science fiction. Personal favorites on my author radar became Brian Aldiss and Poul Anderson for their sweeping stories that not only covered vast stretches of time but demonstrated an amazing knowledge of history and human behavior. And sobering books like John Brunner's *Stand on Zanzibar* (1968), one of the first books to visualize in media-byte fragments a near future plagued with too many people, showed that SF was about much more than just aliens and rocketships.

CREATING THE INTERACTIVE MACHINE (2)

The Convergence of Hardware and Software

I write and illustrate on my trusty computer. I travel the World Wide Web and keep in touch with friends and colleagues by e-mail. I both praise and curse the machine that has come to dominate work and play by the end of the twentieth and beginning of the twenty-first century. The dream of a computing device that could interact with its user in real time essentially began with Jay Forrester, team leader on a project to create a flight simulator for the Navy in 1944. Project Whirlwind, as it was called, became operational in 1951. Filling the area of a small house, it had roughly the power of a 1980s vintage TRS-80 computer.

Like many other scientific achievements, Whirlwind's survival depended on its military potential. After Soviets tested an A-bomb in 1949, soldiers and politicians felt they needed a system to track foreign airplanes that could be carrying a bomb. Whirlwind became SAGE—Semi-Automatic Ground Environment—a continent-spanning network of 23 centers that could track 400 airplanes at once. Although SAGE was never used in combat, it spawned both the hardware and software revolutions that led to modern computers.

SAGE research found its way to IBM. One spin-off yielded the automatic ticketing system first used by American Airlines. The Pentagon funded research on command and control systems that became ARPA—Advanced Research Projects Agency. J. C. R. Licklider (1915–1990) headed the agency and had a vision for a system of interactive terminals he called "thinking centers." He outlined his concept in a 1958 article called "Man Machine Symbiosis." At MIT he developed project MAC in 1963, which would eventually evolve into the first online community of scientists. He proposed a nationwide "Intergalactic Computer Network," which his successor, Robert W. Taylor, proceeded to build in 1966.

The interactive aspect of SAGE research led Kenneth Olsen and Harlan Anderson to found DEC (Digital Equipment Corporation) in 1957. In 1960 their first computer, PDP-1, became a hit with scientists and engineers who could, for a mere $120,000, interact with a room-sized computer via CRT screen easily and efficiently. Steadily shrinking microchips ultimately led to units of truly desktop size that weighed only 250 pounds. By the early seventies hobbyists could build their own minicomputers using the fruits of DEC's labors. In 1975, inspired by an article in *Popular Electronics,* Bill Gates and Paul Allen wrote the computer language BASIC and founded Microsoft to market it to the general public. Steve Wozniak and Steve Jobs created the user-friendly Apple operating system in 1976.

Meanwhile, Xerox was busily developing the modern desktop computing environment of stand-alone personal computer, graphical user interface, laser printing, WYSIWYG (What You See Is What You Get) word-processing systems, and more, using funds from ARPA. In the early eighties a system called Arpanet developed, which, through the National Science Foundation, became NSFnet in 1986, uniting university scientists in a computing network that would go public as the Internet. In 1985 Microsoft introduced Windows 1.0, and the interactive computer entered the mass market and the middle-class working world.

Virtual Realities and Cyberpunk

In 1983 Bruce Bethke wrote a story called "Cyberpunk" for *Amazing Stories.* Gardner Dozois used the term to describe a subgenre of SF, often set in a relatively near future, where key elements include man-machine hybridization and exploration of "virtual realities." In fact, when we speak of cyberspaces and nets and VR we are borrowing language cyberpunk writers pioneered. "Cyber" is a shortened form of cybernetics, a science that compares living to mechanical systems. Cyberpunk universes are often controlled by industrial and political organizations dependent on information networks. The "punk" part of the term refers to eighties rock and roll. Protagonists tend to be young, streetwise, aggressive, and often antiestablishment. A film like *Blade Runner* (1982) provides a stage image of the milieu a reader can expect. William Gibson's *Neuromancer* (1984) is described by Hartwell and Cramer as "the primary cyberpunk text" (*The Ascent of Wonder,* 1994, p. 39).

Some critics, even among fellow writers, felt many stories in the category to be too formulaic. Orson Scott Card said, "Splash some drugs onto a brain-and-microchip interface, mix it up with some vague sixties-style counterculture, and then use really self-conscious, affected language, and you've got cyberpunk" (Clute and Nicholls, 1995, p. 289).

Although some say the subgenre didn't survive into the nineties, good writers absorbed what was worthwhile. Vernor Vinge, author of *A Deepness in the Sky* (1999) and the Hugo-winning *A Fire in the Deep* (1992), liberally employs man-machine hybrids and genetic engineering in his stories. Gregory Benford does the same in a series of novels, beginning with *In the Ocean of Night* (1977), where he depicts the universe as a battleground between organic and mechanical life forms.

THE SECRETS OF LIFE

The Genetic Code

While discoveries in physics tended to dominate the first part of the twentieth century, the nature of living systems jumped to the foreground in the second half, propelled to a great degree by the clarification of gene structure and the mechanism of heredity. James Watson (1928–) and Francis

Crick (1916–) startled the world in 1953 with their proposed structure for deoxyribonucleic acid, DNA, tagged as the genetic chemical in the previous decade.

Others also were working on the problem, including the chemist Linus Pauling (1901–1994) and Rosalind Franklin (1920–1958), who had X-rayed the molecule and was trying to work out structure from her 2-D images. But Watson and Crick, working with cardboard and wire models, data on chemical bond distances, and some flashes of insight, hit upon the structure first: two strands of sugar-phosphate chains wound about each other in a double helix connected by pairs of purine and pyrimidine bases locked together with hydrogen bonds. Looking at their final model of the structure, Watson claimed, "It was too pretty not to be true" (Haven and Clark, 1999). The structure immediately implied a method of replication: when the hydrogen bonds between the helices broke, each single strand could serve as the template for creating its missing half.

During the fifties and sixties researchers worked out the details of how the genetic message became translated into functional cell machinery and metabolic reactions. Through the work of Jacques Monod (1910–1976), Francois Jacob (1920–), and others, a sister molecule, ribonucleic acid (RNA)—in several different forms—was found to copy relevant portions of the nuclear DNA, and transfer it to cellular structures called ribosomes. Ribosomes are construction sites where messenger RNA (from the nucleus) serves as the template for protein manufacture. Proteins become both the architectural structure of the cell and enzyme facilitators of chemical reactions.

Although even the simplest organism's genetic code is unbelievably complex, Francis Collins, head of the Human Genome Project, and Craig Venter, head of a private firm, Celera Genomics, announced jointly in 2000 that they had decoded a "rough draft" of the entire human genetic code that was 91% complete (*Discover,* January 2001). Approximately 38,000 genes define a human being—an imposing number, but still only 5,000 genes more than mustard weed. Scientists are now learning that much of the so-called junk DNA, which does not code for specific proteins, may represent previously hidden layers of genomic information crucial to the operation and regulation of conventional genes. These insights point toward exciting research for the next century.

Conquering Diseases

Control of disease in the twentieth century followed in the wake of discoveries in microbiology, molecular biology, and chemistry. In 1928, Alexander Fleming (1881–1955), in a famous bit of serendipity, discovered penicillin as a contaminant on some staphylococcus colonies he was growing. Drug companies developed it for general use just in time for World War II. Gerhard Domagk's (1895–1954) 1932 discovery of sulfanilamide, the first sulfa drug, added to the antibacterial arsenal. In 1943, Selman Waksman (1888–1973) found another substance from mold that proved effective against the tuberculosis bacterium. The nature of viruses, first discovered in 1898 by Martinis Beijerinck (1851–1931), became clearer during the thirties. These almost-living fragments of nucleic acid and protein that hijack cell machinery to make copies of themselves still prove difficult to control. And now prions—protein fragments even smaller than viruses—appear to cause certain neurological diseases like scrapie and "mad cow disease" (Suplee, 2000).

Nevertheless, scientists learned to harness the body's own defenses to fight back. Jonas Salk (1914–1995) and Albert Sabin (1906–1993) made my generation safe from polio with their vaccines. Vaccinations and sound health practices managed to eliminate smallpox completely in 1977—assuming that we, as a species, are smart enough not to make war with a few small samples set aside in the United States and Russia. One consequence, of course, is that human populations have soared. At over 6 billion people and rising, human populations threaten to strain planetary resources to the limits and reconfigure long-established ecologies. Human effluents appear to be altering global climate.

The Chemistries of Life

Scientists have probed life's operations and origins and rendered them less mysterious. Building on the work of Aleksandr Oparin (1894–1980) in 1953, Stanley Miller (1930–) showed that amino acids, the building blocks of proteins, could be formed quite readily from methane, ammonia, and hydrogen—chemicals prevalent on a young Earth—and electrical discharges. Microfossils from ancient rocks demonstrate that life started soon after the Earth cooled—within the first billion years of its existence. Ancient microbes with anaerobic, mineral-based metabolisms (the Archaea) teamed up with bacteria-like forms to build the "oxygen dynamo" eukaryotic cells of all modern plants and animals about 1.75 billion years ago.

The biochemistry of these modern, patchwork cells were clarified in stages. In the thirties, Robert Hill (1899–1991) showed that the oxygen produced during photosynthesis in plants comes from the water used in the process. Melvin Calvin (1911–1997), during the 1980s, worked out the details of the so-called dark reaction in photosynthesis that converts carbon dioxide to sugars. Other researchers unraveled the details of cellular metabolism in the cell's powerhouses, the mitochondria, which may actually be adopted bacteria from the ancient symbiosis of the first living kingdoms (3).

In the latter half of the twentieth century, the questioning human brain has also learned some things about its own operating schematics, although much still remains a mystery. Research in the sixties on animals and people with brain damage showed that regions of the brain specialize in certain functions, although with integrated connections to other areas. In the eighties and nineties research advanced in three areas: computer models of brain function, the chemistry at nerve junctions, and imaging techniques (like PET scans) that show what areas of the brain are active during certain mental processes. Current research has begun to focus on the nature of consciousness itself (Suplee, 2000).

THE HUMANIZING OF SCIENCE FICTION

Technology-heavy stories of early science fiction left center stage in the second half of the twentieth century to more thoughtful and literary explorations of science, society, and the nature of mind and consciousness. Some of this resulted from New Wave experiments, some from the influence of a turbulent social and political milieu, and some, almost certainly, from the maturing of women writers who took an interest in the genre.

Women in SF

Many women entered the previously male-dominated SF arena in the sixties and seventies and provided well-written novels set in futures with altered sex roles for their human characters. A few sample titles include *Picnic in Paradise* (1968) by Joanna Russ, *The Left Hand of Darkness* (1969) by Ursula K. LeGuin, *Motherlines* (1978) by Suzy McKee Charnas, *The Heritage of Hastur* (1975) by Marion Zimmer Bradley, and *The Women Men Don't See* (1976) by James Tiptree, Jr.—aka Alice B. Sheldon. Tiptree, thought to be a male writer by her followers for a decade (1967–1977), wrote with considerable irony and a consistent fatalism. In an amazing novella called "Houston, Houston, Do You Read?" a three-man solar expedition of the late twentieth century inadvertently passes through a time warp that takes them several hundred years into the future. Their ship disabled, the male astronauts are rescued by a ship crewed by women (although some, at first, appear superficially to be men). The men eventually discover that the male sex has been found to be not only unnecessary, but considered dangerous to the survival of the species. Much of her best work has been collected in *Her Smoke Rose Up Forever: The Great Years of James Tiptree, Jr.* (1990).

Ursula LeGuin wrote *The Dispossessed: An Ambiguous Utopia* (1974), an unusual blend of SF with the earlier utopian novel tradition. In her story a brilliant physicist from an isolated and somewhat backward planet visits the rich mother planet, Urras, and sees the need for breaking down the walls of hatred, distrust, and philosophy that separate his two worlds. In 2003 LeGuin was given a Grand Master Award by her peers for her body of work, which includes both SF and fantasy. Her series of Hainish novels postulate a universe in which star systems in our part of the Milky Way galaxy were seeded by an ancient race called the Hain. She explores the interactions of long-separated worlds and, using her considerable knowledge of anthropology, bares the underlying assumptions of our society for the reader.

Connie Willis (1945–), who has now garnered more Nebula awards than any other science fiction writer, writes with humor and irony, and comes armed with a great knowledge of history (see suggestions for using her work in Chapter 9). Her career blossomed after a short story called "Daisy in the Sun" (1979), about a young girl coming of age in the last days before the sun goes nova. *The Encyclopedia of Science Fiction* says that in the best of her stories and novels "a steel felicity of mind and style appears effortlessly married to a copious empathy."

Ecology Awareness and an "Up-Your-Taboos" Attitude

Stranger in a Strange Land (1961), written by Robert Heinlein, the war-hero-engineer and technofiction master from the Golden Age, achieved mainstream cult status—especially among college students—in the sixties. Heinlein shifted the pattern of his earlier fiction and wrote a fascinating tale about a young boy—Valentine Michael Smith—who was the sole survivor of an ill-fated, first mission to Mars. Smith was born on the two-year journey there and was an infant when the expedition reached Mars. He was discovered 25 years later, along with an ancient Martian Civilization, by the next ship to reach Mars. Smith, human in body but Martian by upbringing, came to Earth naive but possessed of superior mental abilities, providing Heinlein with wonderful opportunities for a cynical and satirical look at our society. He managed to weave ritual cannibalism, promiscuous sex, suicide, anarchy, and the growth of a Martian-inspired religion into a humorous and idea-packed volume just right for a generation looking to change the world.

Another science fiction tale that broke free from genre status to reach mainstream popularity, *Dune* (1965), written by Frank Herbert, tells the story of Paul Atreides, a young prince trying to survive to reclaim his inheritance in a future, space-faring civilization. After an assassination attempt, Paul and his mother escape to Dune, a desert planet richly described and peopled with nomadic Fremen who teach Paul how to survive in its extreme environment. Herbert took such care in describing the economics surrounding the addictive spice, melange, and the interactions of the various plants, animals, and humans on Dune that the word "ecology" rose sharply on readers' awareness barometers. David Hartwell claims, "It is quite possible that the emergence of ecology as a popular idea in the mass media in the late sixties and early seventies can be traced to the impact of this one science fiction novel on youthful opinion-shapers" (*Age of Wonders,* p. 32). (See Chapter 8: "Of Spice and Sandworms.")

David Brin, one of SF's scientist-writers, highlighted environmental themes in *Earth* (1990). Set in the near future, the novel chronicles the attempts of scientists to keep a miniature black hole (a space-time singularity left over from the origins of the universe) from destroying the Earth's core. In the process the reader sees a familiar world, but one transformed by overpopulation, a degraded environment, and runaway greenhouse overheating.

Ecological studies also opened up possibilities of consciously altering a planet to make it more friendly to our version of life. Writers, still looking longingly at Mars, conceived of ways to terraform it—make it more Earth-like—and examine the ethics and consequences of such a procedure. Notable in this category is Kim Stanley Robinson's series *Red Mars* (1992), *Green*

Mars (1993), and *Blue Mars* (1996). The novels span several centuries over which Mars is transformed, exploring the conflicts between Earth and various Martian factions struggling to either preserve something of the old Mars or completely remake her.

Pamela Sargent terraformed Venus in her trilogy *Venus of Dreams* (1986), *Venus of Shadows* (1988), and *Child of Venus* (2001). She chose to emphasize the human burdens imposed by the decisions of parents and grandparents on the generations that follow them, staying true to the new scientific discoveries that revealed Venus to be a planet consumed by a runaway greenhouse effect.

Destiny of Man and the Universe

Some writers still tackled big themes on vast time scales, echoing books like Stapledon's *Star Maker*. Golden Age maestro Isaac Asimov built on themes from his Foundation books, ultimately merging that future of galactic empire and rebirth with his nearer-future robot stories. Gregory Benford, David Brin, and Greg Bear (collectively referred to as the "Killer B's" for their prominence in late-twentieth-century SF) each wrote books based on Asimov's future of galactic empire and near-immortal robots working behind the scenes (4).

Benford, professor of physics at the University of California at Irvine, has written a series of novels set in the same fictional "universe" in which organic and inorganic (mechanical) life forms struggle for control on grand scales of both time and space. Examples are *In the Ocean of Night* (1977), *Across the Sea of Suns* (1984), and *Sailing Bright Eternity* (1995). Benford also garnered the Nebula and John W. Campbell Memorial Award for his 1980 novel *Timescape*, about an attempt to change a grim history by communicating across time using tachyons. This book provides one of the best fictional descriptions of scientists at work.

The Killer B's may have to add to their number with Stephen Baxter, another scientist who has made a name for himself writing fiction based on sound science. He has written a trilogy using the same characters (though their fates are different), but postulating different universes. In the first book, *Manifold Time* (2000), humans are alone in the universe. Ex-astronaut Reid Malenfant mounts an expedition to an asteroid with an artifact from the future. He sees humans evolve and adapt until the last glimmers of energy flicker out. He believes a less depressing future is possible and sets out to create it. In *Manifold Space* (2001) the Fermi Paradox (5) is solved when evidence of alien life shows up in the asteroid belt. Unfortunately, the mechanical aliens are fleeing a wave of destruction generated by the expansion of another species along our galactic arm and an aging Malenfant must try to stem the tide. *Manifold Origin* (2002) looks at a lonely universe where human evolution pursued different paths in parallel universes. An intelligence from near the end of time mixes the results on a customized red moon to try and create a better future.

As science has answered some questions, certain science fictions have become obsolete or at least colored by the societal assumptions of their writers. The new questions scientists inevitably must ask after solving one enigma lead to revisiting old themes of meaning and existence, but also offer glimpses of previously unimagined frontiers.

MEDIA SCIENCE FICTION AND POP CULTURE

It's hard to talk about the literature of SF without mentioning the "sci-fi" that appears in popular TV shows and movies. TV shows and cinema certainly allow their fans to visualize various futures with increasingly sophisticated realism, but they often lack the conceptual depth of SF literature. Robert Heinlein, the popular SF writer, tried to start SF movies on the right track with *Destination Moon* in 1947. Hollywood spent lots of money, followed his script closely, and paid attention to accurate detail. The movie did well. But so did the movies of imitators who spent less money and ignored scientific details. Lots of fluff and junk filled the marketplace for over a decade. Nothing comparable to *Destination Moon* surfaced again until Arthur C. Clarke and Stanley Kubrick's collaboration produced *2001: A Space Odyssey*.

In the sixties, a low-budget TV show called *Star Trek* appeared that gave SF readers—and scientists—the embodiment of that sense of wonder and a positive human future that John Campbell had espoused. *Star Trek* presented something of a utopian future where a mature, enlightened human Federation charges about the galaxy in the starship *Enterprise* in search of new life forms, urging them to conform to humane standards of conduct. For the most part, various long-standing SF ideas were lifted (things like warp drives, mass/energy transporters, etc.) and used to move a plot that highlighted issues of conduct and ideals. Although the show was canceled after a brief run—in spite of a major letter-writing campaign by fans—books, movies, and other series centered on the "*Star Trek* universe" still abound four decades later. Another letter-writing campaign successfully urged President Ford to name the first space shuttle the *Enterprise* (see footnote 5, Chapter 1).

In the seventies, George Lucas startled movie-goers with the fantastic images in *Star Wars*. *Star Wars*–style movies are essentially Westerns-in-Space, in the space opera tradition of E. E. Smith. Good guys successfully battle bad guys, and the major good guy woos and wins the spirited princess. Nevertheless, the techno-gadgets and space drives used in these popular forms of science fiction can serve as hooks to get students to pay attention to the science that underlies the fictional technology.

I hope the last three chapters have provided a foundation for relating science fiction to the scientific discoveries that inspired it. Obviously, I could only provide a sketch of both the history of science and the literature of science fiction, but you should be able to refer to the material here and at least gain some insight into the context of any science fiction you may want to use in the classroom. You may also find some exciting possibilities in tracing the history of scientific missteps or mistaken theories that will help students realize the tentative and ongoing nature of science and how *exciting, world-shattering,* and *humbling* the search for understanding can be.

My focus has been on science fiction literature, largely because SF writers tend to be more careful about the science than TV, movies, or other popular venues. But sometimes there may be great value in pointing out the absurdities of poorly done SF or in using visual media. The next chapter will show you some options before diving into the concrete classroom activities using SF literature.

NOTES

(1) The initial theory of asteroid bombardment developed out of the discovery of Louis and Walter Alvarez of a thin layer containing high amounts of iridium at the Cretaceous/Tertiary (KT) boundary. Iridium is common in meteorites but not in the crust of the Earth. This telltale iridium layer was subsequently found in many locations worldwide. It took several years to find a crater of the right size and age to serve as the "smoking gun" that convinced a majority of Earth scientists that the theory was most likely true. Walter Alvarez tells the story in *T. rex and the Crater of Doom* (Princeton University Press, 1997).

(2) Information for this section comes from Mitchell Waldrop's article "The Origins of Personal Computing" in *Scientific American* 285, no. 6, 2001.

(3) Lynn Margulis, a professor of biology at Boston University, is perhaps the prime advocate for this concept. In fact, in a recent book she wrote with Dorion Sagan, *Acquiring Genomes: A Theory of the Origin of Species* (Basic Books, 2002), she contends that these species amalgamations may contribute more to speciation than random mutations.

(4) Greg Bear's *Foundation and Chaos* (1998) followed Benford's *Foundation's Fear* (1997). Brin wrote *Foundation's Triumph* (1999).

(5) Enrico Fermi (1901–1954) is alleged to have asked one day at Los Alamos in the late 1940s, "If there are aliens, where are they?" His contention was that if any civilization reached a level of technology capable of colonizing other star systems they could do so in a relatively short time (geologically speaking)—say, 100 million years. Therefore, since we don't see evidence of them, they don't exist (or we are the first—or technological civilizations are short-lived and interstellar distances too great). (Also, see Chapter 8.)

REFERENCES

Ballard, J. G. *The Drowned World* (1962). Garden City, NY: Doubleday, 1965.

Ballard, J. G. *The Wind from Nowhere* (1962). Garden City, N Y: Doubleday, 1965.

Baxter, Stephen. *Manifold Origin*. New York: Ballantine Publishing Group, 2002.

Baxter, Stephen. *Manifold Space*. New York: Ballantine Publishing Group, 2001.

Baxter, Stephen. *Manifold Time*. New York: Ballantine Publishing Group, 2000.

Benford, Gregory. *Across the Sea of Suns*. New York: Bantam Books, 1984.

Benford, Gregory. *In the Ocean of Night*. New York: Bantam Books, 1977.

Benford, Gregory. *Sailing Bright Eternity*. New York: Bantam Books, 1995.

Benford, Gregory. *Timescape*. New York: Bantam Books, 1980.

Bethke, Bruce. "Cyberpunk." *Amazing Stories*, 1983.

Blish, James. *Welcome to Mars* (1967). New York: Avon Books, 1983.

Bova, Ben. *Mars*. New York: Bantam Books, 1992.

Bradbury, Ray. *The Martian Chronicles* (1950). New York: Bantam Books, 1962.

Bradley, Marion Zimmer. *The Heritage of Hastur* (1975). Boston: Gregg Press, 1977.

Brin, David. *Earth*. New York: Bantam Books, 1990.

Brunner, John. *Stand on Zanzibar*. New York: Doubleday & Co., 1968.

Charnas, Suzy McKee. *Motherlines*. New York: Berkley Publishing Group, 1978.

Clarke, Arthur C. *Sands of Mars* (1951). New York: Harcourt Brace Jovanovich, 1967.

Clute, John, and Peter Nicholls. *The Encyclopedia of Science Fiction*. New York: St. Martin's Griffin, 1995.

D'agnese, Joseph. "The Year in Science." *Discover* 22, no. 1, January 2001: 49–69.

Ellison, Harlan. *Dangerous Visions*. New York: Doubleday & Co., 1967.

Gibson, William. *Neuromancer*. New York: Berkley Publishing Corp., 1984.

Hartwell, David. *Age of Wonders, Exploring the World of Science Fiction*. New York: Walker & Co., 1984.

Hartwell, David G., and Kathryn Cramer, eds. *The Ascent of Wonder: The Evolution of Hard SF*. New York: TOR, 1994.

Haven, Kendall, and Donna Clark. *100 Most Popular Scientists for Young Adults*. Englewood, CO: Libraries Unlimited, 1999.

Heinlein, Robert A. *Red Planet* (1949). New York: Ballantine Books, 1977.

Heinlein, Robert A. *Stranger in a Strange Land*. New York: Avon Books, 1961.

LeGuin, Ursula. *The Dispossessed: An Ambiguous Utopia*. New York: Harper & Row, 1974.

LeGuin, Ursula. *The Left Hand of Darkness*. New York: Harper & Row, 1969.

Ochoa, George, and Melinda Corey. *The Timeline Book of Science*. New York: Ballantine Books, 1995.

Robinson, Kim Stanley. *Blue Mars*. New York: Bantam Books, 1996.

Robinson, Kim Stanley. *Green Mars*. New York: Bantam Books, 1993.

Robinson, Kim Stanley. *Red Mars*. New York: Bantam Books, 1992.

Russ, Joanna. *Picnic in Paradise*. New York: Berkeley Publishing Group, 1968.

Sargent, Pamela. *Child of Venus*. New York: HarperCollins Publishers, 2001.

Sargent, Pamela. *Venus of Dreams*. New York: HarperCollins Publishers, 1986.

Sargent, Pamela. *Venus of Shadows*. New York: HarperCollins Publishers, 1988.

Sturgeon, Theodore. "The Man Who Lost the Sea" in *The Golden Helix,* New York: Carroll and Graf, 1959.

Suplee, Curt. *Milestones of Science*. Washington, DC: National Geographic, 2000.

Tiptree, James, Jr. *The Women Men Don't See* (1976), "Houston, Houston, Do You Read?" (1976) in *Her Smoke Rose Up Forever: The Great Years of James Tiptree, Jr.* Sauk City, WI: Arkham House Publishers, 1990.

Vinge, Vernor. *A Deepness in the Sky.* New York: TOR, 1999.

Vinge, Vernor. *A Fire in the Deep.* New York: TOR, 1992.

Willis, Connie. "Daisy in the Sun" (1979) in *The 1980 Annual World's Best SF*. New York: Daw Books, 1980, p. 136.

ADDITIONAL READING

Herbert, Brian. *Dreamer of Dune, the Biography of Frank Herbert.* New York: TOR, 2003.

CONCEPTUAL BREAKTHROUGHS

Aristotle and the Greek faith in rationalism
"Sense perception is the
only means of human knowledge"

Greek thought preserved by the Church after the
fall of Rome and by the Muslim "House of Knowledge"

Thomas Aquinas makes "reason"
acceptable with the Catholic Church

Tycho Brahe and others devote their energies to
careful astronomical observations and meticulous records

Copernicus: the measure of "truth"
becomes consistency with observation,
not conformance with orthodoxy

Kepler deduces laws of planetary motions, building on Tycho Brahe's
work; Galileo makes crucial astronomical and physical observations;
Francis Bacon makes rationalism acceptable

Newton quantifies (with the Calculus)
and codifies the basic laws of force and motion

Belief in a "clockwork universe" grows, with God as
the clockmaker

Lavoisier extends quantification and careful observation
to the study of matter in interaction (chemistry)
Dalton and Atomic Theory

Physics/Chemistry/Math

- Unification of electricity and magnetism
- Periodicity in chemical behavior
- Variability of time and $E = MC^2$
- Quantum theory
- Black Holes and the search for GUTs
- Probability, fractals, chaos theory

Earth and Space Sciences

- Uniformitarianism
- Principal of stratigraphy
- Absolute dating
- Plate techtonics
- Spectroscopy
- Red shift and the expanding universe
- Cepheid variables and other tools for measuring the size of the universe

Life Sciences/Medicine

- Theory of evolution by natural selection
- Nature of genetic code
- Biochemistry of life/ origin of life
- Punctuated equilibrium/ evolution by symbiotic merger
- Principals of ecology/ Gaia concept
- Understanding the role of microorganisms in disease

TECHNOLOGIES

Railroads	Canal building/surveying	Animal husbandry
Steam engine	Telescopes	Crop improvement
Balloon flight	Navigation	Genetic engineering
Electric power	GPS technologies	Designer drugs
Plastics and other new materials	Rocketry	Wildlife management
Computers	Powered flight	Software evolution
Nuclear power plants	Mining technology	Life extension techniques
Suspension bridges	Weather forecasting	Advertising strategies
Gasoline engine	Fossil fuel exploitation	Artificial intelligence
Photography, etc.	Space travel, etc.	Medical technologies, etc.

Figure 4.2. Overview of scientific advances and the growth of technology (*left*); a timeline of scientific discoveries and SF literature (*right*).

Milestones in Science and the Literature of the Fantastic

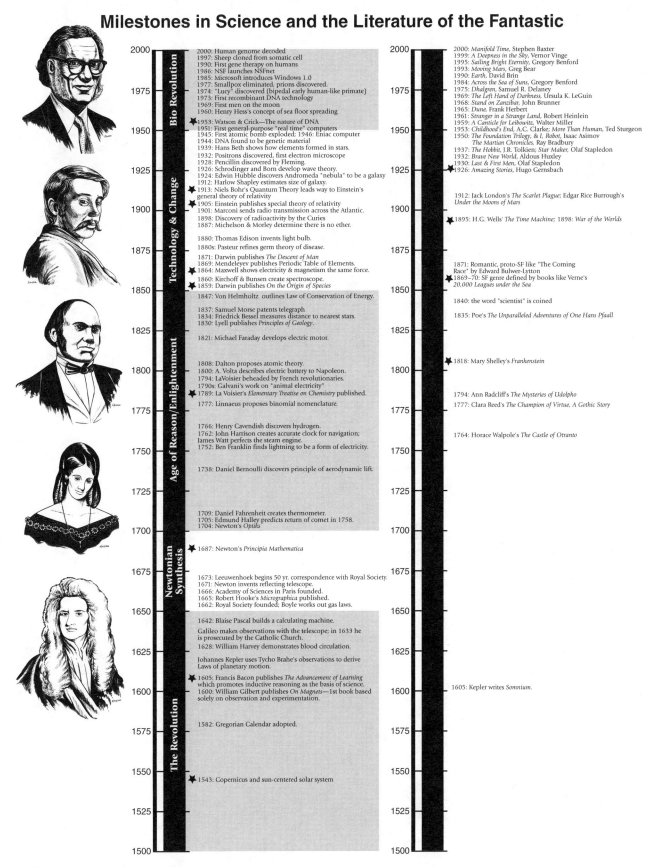

Figure 4.2. (*Continued*)

CHAPTER 5

What Kind of Science Fiction Is Right for You?

"When a distinguished but elderly scientist states that something is possible, he is almost certainly right. When he states that something is impossible, he is very probably wrong."
Arthur C. Clarke, *Profiles of the Future*

In the past, a person in search of fiction might read a book, attend a play, or listen to a poet or wandering minstrel. The written symbols or spoken words of the artist metamorphosed in the translator's brain to create a hybrid, entertaining—perhaps even enlightening—experience. Today, we often know *exactly* the images we are meant to experience because the visual illusions created for TV and movies mimic reality to near-perfection. Your students can probably name more TV shows and movies than book titles. You would be foolish *not* to make use of their power as a teaching tool, which is why I am sampling some of what's available in "Medialand" in this chapter.

And yet . . . I'm hoping in the end you will choose to sample the literary roots (and current blossoms) of SF as a teaching tool, which is what most of the rest of the book is about. Discovering literary SF makes students work a bit harder to manufacture their own visual interpretations, but it offers richer fare than what can be produced by a few million dollars and a couple of hours of their attention span. But let's look at some of the things available in media "sci-fi," and you can decide . . .

A CLASSIC RADIO BROADCAST: WAR OF THE WORLDS

Families no longer huddle in front of the radio to listen to the adventures of Superman, the Shadow, the Flash, and other characters who brought adventure and mystery into their lives. The form was all but extinct when I was growing up, but I did enjoy many episodes as "classic radio broadcasts." Spoken stories stir the listener's imagination in unique ways, not possible when the visual element is provided gratis. Turn down the lights and let the power of a master storyteller pluck chords of wonder not unlike those strummed by shamans over flickering firelight for 100,000 years. Thus I was gratified to read an article in *Science Scope* by Margaret E. Bolick, who described using Orson Welles' classic broadcast of H. G. Wells' *The War of the Worlds* to ignite student interest in studying the planets of our solar system (1).

Bolick has shown that students respond enthusiastically to this once panic-inducing broadcast. It is still readily available from several sources, which are listed at the end of the chapter. She has students draw pictures of Martians as described in the broadcast, compare their structure and appearance to humans, and relate each life form to the characteristics of their planet of origin. Students also can pick a planet in the solar system and design a life form consistent with the conditions on the planet. Bolick involves them in writing stories of how their creations might survive on planets other than their homeworld. Many of these exercises parallel some I've suggested in Chapter 7 under "Aliens in Deep Space and Planet Building."

THE TELEVISION GENERATION

They Just Keep on Trekking

In the early 1990s educators at Purdue's Physics Outreach Program surveyed 30,000 students in the Indiana and Chicago area and asked who—other than parents and teachers—is most influential in their lives in promoting science. The runaway first choices were characters from the original *Star Trek* TV series and *Star Trek: The Next Generation*. Both these series are still shown regularly as reruns along with two other spinoffs: *Deep Space Nine* and *Star Trek Voyager.* The current TV offering in this apparently immortal future universe is *Star Trek: Enterprise,* which details the beginning of human exploration of space after "first contact" by Vulcan spacefarers. Obviously, many students (and their parents) can easily relate to this resource.

On one level a person could argue that much of *Star Trek* is not really SF at all, because many episodes deal with issues of ethics and human relationships that could have been explored in a contemporary setting. New scientific concepts are not often central to the story being told. But new scientific ideas have been woven into the story line and some care has been taken not to violate known scientific laws or principles without at least explaining away how those laws were circumvented (for exceptions, see notes in the following section regarding scientific errors). Scientific issues explored include things like starship propulsion systems ("warp drive"), black holes, worm holes, neutron stars, time travel, Dyson spheres, matter-energy conversion (transporter technology), matter-antimatter, dark matter, quasars, holograms, artificial intelligence, eugenics, terraforming planets, and the nature and structure of the universe.

Sue Ellen Radhe and Lynn Cole in another *Science Scope* article entitled "Star Trek Physics" suggest a three-step process for using *Star Trek* TV shows in the classroom:

1. Find a show that illustrates the concept.

2. Read what scientists have to say about the issue.

3. Create a simple model to demonstrate the concept.

The first directive is not difficult. Log on to www.startrek.com (2003), follow the Library Link, and you will discover the name, story outline, graphics, film clips, and related links for every episode of every *Star Trek* TV series and movie. For a fairly modest investment, you can have every episode on DVD for a classroom resource. Most cable services offer an SF channel that usually carries each series on a regular basis and/or have regular "Trek-a-thons" that you can videotape.

The second directive is not as hard as it sounds. You don't need to wear out your best horn-rimmed glasses scanning through physics journals or textbooks. The best resources are often titles in the children's library that will give you a solid foundation. You can then move to adult books by science popularizers. Refer to Appendix 1 for a sampling of these, along with a few titles that specifically address the science in *Star Trek* and other popular movie and TV blockbusters.

Again, the children's section of your library can provide excellent resources for fulfilling the requirement for a simple model. Books with "how to" in the title can be invaluable. Good choices are *How the Universe Works: 100 Ways Parents and Kids Can Share the Secrets of the Universe,* or *Astronomy for Every Kid: 101 Easy Experiments That Really Work.*

Star Trek does offer something else common to much science fiction: a hopeful view of the future. Yes, there is still much murder, mayhem, betrayal, and danger—the tools for creating drama and conflict—but the human race has survived the trials of its Earth-bound youth and explores alien cultures and strange worlds with enthusiasm and a moral code of conduct at the boundaries of the "last frontier."

Other TV Fare

You will find, mostly on the "Sci-fi" channel and TNN, an assortment of SF series mixed with horror, pseudoscience, and fantasy. Star Trek's creator, Gene Roddenberry, is also credited with the concept behind *Earth: Final Conflict,* a series about human interaction with a technologically superior race that has supposedly come to Earth as friends and benefactors, but has ulterior motives as well. This series seems less concerned with new scientific concepts than with establishing a rather dark, dramatic tone, but the whole notion of what would happen to humans and their civilization if they encountered a more advanced species provides material for reflection. (Of course, in the true Campbellian tradition, humans in this show have some special features that the aliens really admire and can't do without).

The *X-files* has been quite popular, but deals essentially with pseudoscience presented in Gothic tones. You certainly could use an episode or two to help point out the difference between science and wish fulfillment masquerading in a lab coat. Sometimes people want to retain wonder and mystery in their lives so badly that they will accept too many unfounded claims without a sufficiently critical eye. The *Skeptical Inquirer,* a magazine published by the Committee for the Scientific Investigation of Claims of the Paranormal, is a good resource for critical analyses of pseudoscientific claims.

TV (and movie) SF is, in general, more prone to certain kinds of scientific error—sometimes in the name of dramatic effect. Here are a few classic scientific muffs to look out for and point out to science students:

- "Parsecs" used as a unit of velocity and not distance (this turned up in *Star Wars*).

- The confusion of weight and mass (astronauts can't shove a spaceship out of the way because it is weightless).

- Faster-than-light (FTL) drives with no explanation as to how they are breaking Einstein's speed limit.

- Audible explosions/engine noise in space.

- Finding magical, unknown "rays" within the electromagnetic spectrum.

- Phaser or other electromagnetic "beams" visible in the near-vacuum of space.

- Aliens lusting after human women (or vice versa).

- Fertile, interspecies hybrids aplenty.

- Pressure domes suffering small punctures that result in cyclonic winds as air escapes.

- Giant bugs or other invertebrates (that would collapse under their own weight if scaled up to dinosaurian sizes).

- Flying humans (without major changes in body construction or the proper low-gravity planet on which to fly).

- Telepathy as a way around communication difficulties between species (there is strong evidence that we think with language, which is probably what aliens would do, too).

- Spaceship maneuvers that resemble World War II dogfights and ignore the fact that you must apply thrust to change direction and orientation in space.

- The loss of seat belt technology on the bridge of the *Enterprise* and other ships.

With all its limitations, TV science fiction may provide just the common ground you need to hook student interest and make a connection with the science you want to teach in the classroom.

Hopefully, you will also rachet-up critical skills that will serve students well when evaluating anything they watch, read, or listen to.

CINEMA SCIENCE FICTION

Integration of Science Fiction Movies with the Science Curriculum

Leroy W. Dubeck, Suzanne E. Moshier, and Judith E. Boss collaborated to produce a valuable resource entitled *Fantastic Voyages, Learning Science through Science Fiction Films*. The goal of the book was to provide basic physics and biology instruction, using science fiction movies to provide examples of the concepts. The book is divided into three sections. The first introduces basic physics and astronomy concepts, the second does the same for biological concepts, and the third provides plot descriptions of 32 films. This 1994 book won't have the most recent films on students' radar, but discusses various classics including *2001: A Space Odyssey, The Andromeda Strain, Blade Runner, Forbidden Planet,* and others.

Terence E. Cavanaugh in the March 2002 issue of *Science Scope* describes his use of science fiction films in the classroom. Some of the reasons he cites for using this approach include the following:

- It helps improve students' attitudes toward studying science.

- You can approach a broad range of topics, some of them fairly advanced.

- SF films (and literature) motivate a broader range of students and the dramatic approach facilitates learning.

- Cavanaugh's doctoral research showed these films to be slightly more effective than traditional science videos in improving test scores.

He provides a sample lesson for using the movie *Twister* in the classroom, a student worksheet to be used during the film, and a lab activity on tornado observation that involves having the students fill out a "Storm Chaser's Severe Weather Event Report Form" similar to those used by actual observers in the field.

Science Fiction: Some of It's Now History

Science fiction has been around long enough that it's now possible to compare what writers thought would happen to the actual event. This may provide an opportunity to do several things:

- Integrate science fiction into the history curriculum.

- Discuss how art may influence what people later choose to do or create.

- Explore how scientific advances led to improved technology for creating movie images and how more realistic/elaborate images may impact the viewer.

Destination Moon (1950), loosely based on Robert Heinlein's *Rocket Ship Galileo* (1947), used German rocket expert Hermann Oberth (1894–1989) and Robert Heinlein (an engineer as well as author) as consultants. George Pal produced the film. Told in a documentary-like style, the movie could boast of accurate science, good special effects, and a true sense of wonder—although the plot would not seem especially exciting by today's standards. Heinlein's science showed itself to be more accurate than his speculation that wealthy business interests would be first to put mankind in space. The movie became a commercial success, which, unfortunately, led to many lesser film efforts during the 1950s with much less attention paid to real science, but it may have stimulated a generation of space scientists who later contributed to the actual space effort and subsequent moon landing.

Nearly 20 years later and just prior to the real first moon landing, *2001: A Space Odyssey* (1968) showed a quite different trip to the moon and an expedition to Jupiter. Another science fiction writer/engineer, Arthur C. Clarke, teamed up with Stanley Kubrick to produce a technically accurate, though somewhat darker vision of human space exploration. Humans find a monolith on the moon, which beams a signal home when disturbed to alert some advanced sentience of humanity's coming-of-age. A subsequent, ill-fated Jupiter mission, which suffers from an artificial intelligence named HAL who goes mad, finds a similar monolith on Jupiter. The surviving crew member undergoes a transformation to some higher state of being after transporting through the "star gate" monolith.

For science fiction novices, some of the movie may have seemed a bit fuzzy and somewhat vague. Clarke, in a book written after the film was completed, spells out just what happens more clearly. Kubrick took great pains with special effects. From that standpoint, the movie still holds up well and led to some of the visual breakthroughs created in *Star Wars*.

For a time, in the fifties and sixties, it seemed that science fiction tended to underestimate real progress in science and technology. *2001: A Space Odyssey* overestimated such progress. We still have no artificial intelligences like HAL, commercial moon flights, or manned expeditions to Jupiter. You may wish to discuss with students the cultural and political forces that influence the rate and nature of scientific advancement.

Other Movies of Note

Star Wars (1977) ignited great public interest in science fiction with some interesting regressive repercussions in SF literature. The story itself blends elements of fantasy, spy thrillers, romantic Westerns, comics, and World War II air battles. In SF literature such "space opera" tales dominated much of the Golden Age, but were replaced by more mature themes and ideas later. Advanced special effects brought *Star Wars* visually alive in a way never achieved by prior films. This, combined with the light, upbeat adventure story, made it one of the biggest box office successes ever. Thus, paperback publishing houses rushed to print many more space-opera-style juvenile novels. A teacher could use *Star Wars* to discuss the science behind some of the special effects or to point out some of the scientific errors mentioned in connection with TV science fiction (parsecs as a measure of velocity instead of distance, spaceships making banked course changes, and so forth), but has limited use otherwise.

Likewise, most of the *Star Trek* movies were essentially extensions of a few popular TV episodes or permutations thereof, with the possible exception of the first, *Star Trek the Motion Picture* (1979). The plot line seems derived from two TV episodes: *The Changeling* (1967), written by John Meredith Lucus, and *The Doomsday Machine* (1967), written by Norman Spinrad. A destructive, solar-system-sized cloud, driven by an intelligence at its core that turns out to be a hybrid of the ancient Earth probe *Voyager* and a similar alien device, is racing toward Earth. Only the *Enterprise* and its crew stands in its way. The hybrid intelligence is seeking its creator (which the *Voyager* part believes is on Earth). In the end, the machine and one of the "carbon units" aboard the *Enterprise* fuse into a more complex life form that transcends our mundane universe.

Alien, also shown in 1979, presents more opportunities for teaching, although it's a science fiction/horror hybrid that may be too intense for younger audiences. *Alien* shows a blue-collar crew at work in a grungy, well-used spacecraft (the *Nostromo*) on a commercial mission. They discover a horrific, but biologically believable life form that lays an egg in a crew member. The resulting larval stage bursts forth from the crew member's chest and molts into a voracious adult that picks off the crew one at a time. This lifestyle resembles that of many wasps who parasitize other invertebrates, including butterflies, moths, and spiders, in a similar fashion (although the adult wasp does not eat the species it lays eggs in).

You could easily use the movie as a stimulating lead-in to a study of parasitism and/or insect-style metamorphic life cycles. Students might be required to design other aliens, based on the "lifestyles of the small and ugly" on Earth. Or, you could explore some ethical issues: Do parasitic intelligences have a "right" to survive if it means destroying other intelligent life forms in the process? Could human beings coexist with such a life form, and if so, how?

Other science fiction topics of interest in the movie include artificial life forms and suspended animation techniques. The science officer aboard *Nostromo,* an android passing as human, has been instructed by the Board of Directors to capture alien life forms at any cost, even if that cost includes the lives of the crew. The crew feels that's not in their job description and manage to dispatch said science officer in a messy fashion. The female protagonist, Ripley, uses a suspended animation chamber in a life pod as a last-option method of getting home after destroying the *Nostromo* in an effort to eliminate the alien.

Jurassic Park (1993), again through some of its amazing visual effects, ignited interest in paleontology and genetic engineering. The method of bringing dinosaurs back to life is clever: Find mosquitos trapped in amber whose last meal included dinosaur blood. Extract "fossil" dino DNA from this blood in the mosquito's gut, insert it into the denucleated egg of a modern large bird or reptile, fill in missing genetic information from contemporary birds and reptiles, and voila—wait for the hatching. And, oh yes, make all the dinos infertile so they won't run off and have a sexcapade of evolutionary innovation.

You can build an entire unit on discussing the various problems that must be solved in such a venture:

- How long can DNA remain undegraded in amber?

- How many fossil amber sites exist and how old are they?

- How rare are amber-trapped mosquitos?

- How do you separate dino DNA from other kinds of DNA in the mosquito gut?

- What portion of dinosaurs' 160-million-year history could you successfully sample?

- How can you know which parts and how much of the dino genome are missing and what to replace them with?

- What's involved in creating embryos from somatic cells (cloning)?

One also wonders why the movie wasn't called Cretaceous Park, since many of the "star" dinosaurs, like T. rex and Triceratops, are Cretaceous in age. This could lead into a discussion of how paleontological field work is done, geological time, and other Earth science topics.

Cinematic science fiction, like that offered on TV, is so pervasive and popular that it provides many golden opportunities to spark an interest in science in the classroom. Preview potential movie fare, be selective, and, if time is available, use it to good effect.

LITERARY SF IN THE SHORT FORM

A Brief Guide to SF Short Stories

Don't have time for students to look at entire movies or read entire novels? Consider using some of the excellent short fiction created by imaginative writers now and in the past. Although you might quibble that short stories don't really qualify as "other media," they are a resource easy to overlook if you are not a long-time fan of SF literature.

Magazines

The major magazines in the field of traditional and hard SF include:

- *Analog Science Fiction and Fact,* edited by Dr. Stanley Schmidt, 475 Park Avenue South, 11th floor, New York, NY 10016. Web site: http://www.analogsf.com. The genealogy of this magazine extends back to 1930 when it was called *Astounding. Analog* has a large circulation and fan base and has featured many fine SF writers through the years.

- *The Magazine of Fantasy & Science Fiction,* edited by Gordon Van Gelder, P.O. Box 3447, Hoboken, NJ 07030. Web site: http://www.fsfmag.com/ Another venerable magazine, established in 1949. This magazine has earned a reputation for more literary work, which spans the range from fantasy to science fiction.

- *Isaac Asimov's Science Fiction Magazine,* edited by Gardner Dozois, 475 Park Avenue South, 11th floor, New York, NY 10016. Web site: http://www.asimovs.com. As you may have noted, it shares the same address as *Analog,* a result of common ownership by Davis Publications, Inc. The magazine boasts the highest percentage of award-winning stories, although its circulation is a bit less than that of either of the two magazines mentioned above. It features hard SF compatible with its namesake author.

- *Interzone,* edited by David Pringle, 217 Preston Drove, Brighton, BN1 6FL, UK. Web site: http://www.sfsite.com/interzone/ This British magazine produces an eclectic mix of hard and soft SF with a reputation far greater than its small circulation would indicate (2,000 as opposed to 80,000–100,000 for the large American magazines).

- *Artemis Magazine,* edited by Ian Randal Strock, 1380 East 17 Street, Suite 201, Brooklyn, NY 11230. Web site: http://www.lrcpubs.com/artemismagazine.html. This magazine specializes in "upbeat near-term hard SF involving lunar development or life on the moon."

Anthologies

Gardner Dozois (editor of *Asimov's Magazine*) edits *The Year's Best Science Fiction,* an annual collection published by St. Martin's Press.

David Hartwell has edited, since 1995, *Year's Best SF,* through HarperCollins. In addition, Hartwell, along with Kathryn Cramer, edited a book called *The Ascent of Wonder, The Evolution of Hard SF* (1994, TOR Books), which includes a range of SF stories through the years with commentary on the development of the genre.

Isaac Asimov edited an anthology called *The Hugo Winners* (Doubleday) in 1962, which included early Hugo-winning stories from 1953 to 1961, including "Flowers for Algernon" by Daniel Keyes in 1960 (made into the movie *Charly* in 1968). The Hugo, named after publisher Hugo Gernsback, is an annual fan/amateur award for popular science fiction. The Nebula Award, in contrast, is voted on by fellow professional writers.

Harlan Ellison edited an influential series of 33 stories in 1967 called *Dangerous Visions,* stories considered taboo in popular magazines of the day. The anthology became closely identified with the "New Wave" movement in science fiction (see Chapter 4). "Aye, and Gomorrah . . ." by Samuel R. Delany, "Riders of the Purple Wage" by Phillip Jose Farmer, and "Gonna Roll the Bones" by Fritz Lieber won major awards. *Again, Dangerous Visions* (1972) included work by Joanna Russ and Ursula K. LeGuin.

Individual authors strong in the short story tradition include Connie Willis and Ed Bryant. *Impossible Things* (Bantam, 1993) contains eleven of Willis' stories, eight of which are Hugo and Nebula Award winners or nominees, including "The Last of the Winnebagos" and "Even the Queen." Bryant's collections include "Among the Dead and Other Events Leading up to the Apocalypse" (1973, revised 1974) and "Wyoming Sun" (1980).

Since short stories tend to focus on one key concept or idea, you may find them particularly useful for adding variety to a particular subject area without necessarily building an entire unit around them. I would suggest reading an anthology like *The Ascent of Wonder* to get a feel for some of the best of the genre, then subscribe to a magazine for a year or sample some of the available online SF to see how short fiction could energize your lesson plans.

SCIENCE FICTION ON THE WEB

At this point in time, the Web is a vast resource of information on all topics, but there are few ways to certify the quality of content. Sites abound dealing with science fiction, fantasy, and horror—some suitable for your students and some not. I will list a few dealing with science fiction—particularly the "hard" variety that may be most useful in the science classroom.

Scifi.com

I particularly like www.scifi.com. You can find fact, fiction, and information about current happenings in the world of science fiction writing, reading, and fandom. Wil McCarthy, rocket scientist by day and science fiction writer by desire, writes a regular nonfiction column called *Lab Notes* where he discusses cutting-edge ideas in science. Titles of some of his recent columns include "Nanotech Wonder Plants," "Time Travel and Quantum Chaos," "The Physics of Rollerball," and "Microscopic Ghosts of Mars" (http://www.scifi.com/sfw/current/labnotes.html).

Ellen Datlow, former editor of *Omni Magazine,* edits fiction at scifi.com (scifi.com/scifiction/). Currently the site offers a "classic" short story plus the writing of contemporary authors.

McCarthy's column appears under "Sci Fi Weekly" at the site. "On Air" directs you to various schedules, movies, shows, and events. "Colony" provides message boards, chat areas, and information about joining. Datlow's fiction fare falls under "Presents." You will also find a "Web Guide" to new sites and cool picks and a "Freezone" with various media tools.

Other Sites for Fiction

Oceans of the Mind™ is a quarterly online science fiction magazine with a different theme each quarter. It advertises for "all forms of SF, but no gratuitous or explicit sex and violence." Readers must subscribe. You will find them at www.trantorpublications.com/oceans.htm.

Deep Outside offers fiction "that transcends the limitations and ventures outside, no Sword & Sorcery, porn, excessive violence, or gore." They can be found at www.clocktowerfiction.com.

Speculon SF features "cross-genre stories, cyberpunk, industrial fantasy, golden-age style 'gadget stories,' oddball premises, no horror or very dark fantasy, or gratuitous/excessive violence, gore of any amount, graphic depictions of sex or violence, or hateful/defamatory content." Find them at www.speculon.com.

Would That It Were offers historical SF—SF set in the past between 1830 and 1930 with a flavor harking back to H. G. Wells and Jules Verne. They like "ghost stories, nothing that is porn, obscene, defamatory or otherwise in poor taste." They may be found at www.wouldthatitwere.com.

So, science fiction resources may call to you through many media. When novel-length excursions into the literature—or even short stories—won't work in your situation, feel free to use what radio, TV, movies, and the Web have to offer. And while the rest of this book will primarily address SF literature, you will find that most, if not all, of the suggestions for classroom activities could easily be adapted for use with visual, auditory, or online speculative fiction.

NOTE

(1) Copies of Orson Welles' *War of the Worlds* radio broadcast can be purchased at online sources such as www.amazon.com, old-time.com, or downloaded from www.otr.com/sf.html. Public libraries usually can provide copies as well. Welles, O. "The War of the Worlds" in *The Mercury Theater on the Air*. New York: Columbia Broadcasting System, October 30, 1938.

REFERENCES

Bolick, Margaret E. "Fact or Fiction." *Science Scope* 24, no. 3, November/December 2000.

Cavanaugh, Terence. "Science Fiction and Science." *Science Scope* 25, no. 6, March 2002.

Clute, John, and Peter Nicholls. *The Encyclopedia of Science Fiction*. New York: St. Martin's Griffin, 1993 (update 1995).

Couper, H., and N. Henbest. *How the Universe Works: 100 Ways Parents and Kids Can Share the Secrets of the Universe*. New York: Reader's Digest Association, 1994.

Dubeck, Leroy W., Suzanne E. Moshier, and Judith E. Boss. *Fantastic Voyages, Learning Science through Science Fiction Films*. New York: AIP Press, 1994.

Radhe, Sue Ellen, and Lynn Cole. "Star Trek Physics." *Science Scope* 25, no. 6, March 2002.

Skeptical Inquirer (ISSN 0194-6730), published bimonthly by the Committee for the Scientific Investigation of Claims of the Paranormal, 1310 Sweet Home Road, Amherst, NY 14228.

VanCleave, Janice. *Astronomy for Every Kid, 101 Easy Experiments That Really Work*. New York: John Wiley & Sons, 1991.

CHAPTER 6

SF Resources and Lesson Plans: The Physical Sciences

"Since adventure stories continue to dominate science fiction—with the hero carrying all the action instead of relegating some of his tasks to scientists and technologists (he would need quite a gang of them)—there is good reason for writers to consider Newton's laws to be tyrannical limits which they would love to circumvent."

Amit Goswami, *The Cosmic Dancers*

THE NEWTONIAN UNIVERSE

The laws of force and motion revealed by Newton in the late seventeenth century still govern the activities of our daily lives and must be relearned by each generation. Make the discoveries fresh and new for your students by taking them to very un-Earthly planets and seeing how those laws might affect the creatures (and/or any visiting Earthpersons) who live there. A varied assemblage of planets circles our own sun and many writers have explored the consequences of trying to live on the moon, Venus, Mars, and Jupiter—especially as probes have revealed more about them. Other writers have taken on the harder task of building their own special planets and sharing the consequences of adventures undertaken there with their readers. One master of this latter course, Hal Clement, imagined a world called Mesklin in his story "Mission of Gravity" (*Astounding Science Fiction,* 1953), which you will enjoy exploring (1).

A Mission of Gravity

Mesklin orbits the K5 star, Belne, which in turn circles the larger K7 star, Esstes (2). (See the Hertsprung-Russell diagram in Chapter 7 for star classification by color, size, and luminosity.) Belne crosses Mesklin's sky every 9 minutes at its equator and Belne takes 4.8 Earth years to orbit Esstes. Mesklin rotates on its own axis so quickly that a day is only 18 minutes long. Because it is a methane-ammonia gas giant not too unlike Jupiter, this creates a huge equatorial bulge. Mesklin's pudgy diameter at the equator is 76,800 km, but is only 32,000 km from pole to pole. Its gravity thus ranges from three times Earth-normal at the equator to 700 times Earth-normal at the poles. Summer temperatures reach a balmy −140°, which melts the ammonia snow pack and expands the methane oceans. Earth exploration parties have set up observation stations on Mesklin's two small moons.

Earthmen are especially interested in the native Mesklinites, an intelligent race with a preindustrial, trading culture. They need the Mesklinites to help them out of a jam. An Earth exploratory probe has crash-landed near one of the poles. While Earth technology can allow astronauts to survive and function near the equator, they have no chance at higher latitudes where the ship crashed and 600-g forces prevail. Earthman Charles Lackland made contact with a Mesklinite trader ship's captain named Barlennan, who has agreed to help him find the precise location of the ship and extract its valuable data files in exchange for detailed weather reports and mapping information. (Although Barlennan, being the clever trader he is, ultimately extorts a little more from Lackland near journey's end.)

As one might assume, Mesklinite biology reflects the harsh conditions of Mesklin. Mesklinites are small (35–40 cm long with a 5-cm diameter) and flattened rather like a centipede. They have eighteen pairs of legs ending in sucker-like feet to help keep them anchored to the surface. Falling is usually a fatal experience in Mesklin's gravity. A forward pair of appendages equipped with pincers manipulates objects. The Mesklinites see with four eyes clustered around a mandible-like mouth. They have no lungs, but absorb hydrogen directly from the atmosphere. They produce sound from the very low to the ultrasonic. They possess a tough outer exoskeleton that could easily support a human (balancing on one foot).

For your purposes in teaching the physical sciences, Barlennan's journey from equator to pole will provide many opportunities for exploring Newton's laws in an alien context. I will outline a few possibilities, which you can adapt to your purposes.

Newton's Laws on Mesklin

An Inclined Plane Problem

In Chapters 7 and 8, early in their journey from Mesklin's equator north to the crash site, during a portage with an Earth-made "tank" from one arm of the methane sea to the other, Barlennan and his crew encounter a city built within a bowl-shaped valley. Boulders ring the rim of the valley and the city inhabitants had built a series of trenches from rim to valley floor. The urban Mesklinites live in the resulting "walls" between the trenches. The valley floor serves as a large common area/plaza. With some unease on Earthman Lackland's part, the explorers descend a trench to begin trading in the plaza. All goes well until the city dwellers decide they want the "talking box" (radio) through which Barlennan speaks to Lackland. When Barlennan won't trade, the locals launch a boulder down the trench leading to the tank.

The distance from rim to plaza is approximately a half mile along the slope of the trench. Gravity at this point on Mesklin is three times Earth normal. The author describes the rim as "far above," but offers no precise distance from rim to valley floor. The boulder is approximately half the size of the tank. A 2,200-pound (9,800-Newton) boulder would weigh 6,600 pounds at this point on Mesklin (equivalent to 29,400 Newtons). Making some assumptions about the vertical drop from the rim and the slope of the valley, you might explore this situation as a vector problem and try to determine the speed of the boulder when it reaches the bottom of the ramp or the time it will take it to arrive. How do the speeds and times you calculate compare to the response time the expedition seems to have in the book?

Force and Motion: Dropping Objects on Mesklin

Much later (Chapter 17), near the end of their journey, a group of Mesklinites must ascend 300 feet up a rubble-strewn slope, then haul one crew member and supplies up a cliff face with a hoist. They must accomplish this feat at 600 times Earth's gravity. As an experiment, they push a "bullet-sized" pebble over the edge of the cliff and observe the results: ". . . the pebble simply vanished. There was a short note like a breaking violin string as it clove the air, followed a split second later by a sharp report as it struck the ground below."

Three hundred feet is 91.4 meters. A 30-gram pebble (a little over an ounce) equals 0.030 kilograms. Assuming Mesklin's acceleration due to gravity is 5,880 m/sec^2 (600 × 9.8 m/sec^2), you can calculate the force with which the pebble hits the ground ($F = ma$) or, with some manipulations of the basic equation, the speed of the pebble when it hits the ground (time equals the square root of twice the distance fallen divided by the acceleration due to gravity).

Simple Machines

Simple machines like the lever, pulley, wheel and axle, inclined plane, wedge, and screw make work easier by creating a mechanical advantage (mechanical advantage = resistance force/effort force). Often, the resistance force is the weight of an object to be moved. In Chapter 13, "Slip of the Tongue," some natives, sailing gliders, drop spear-like missiles that stick in the ground and block the expedition's passage. After a truce is made, Barlennan and crew must remove the obstacles. Lackland shows them how to make a "differential hoist" out of a series of pulleys. Have students diagram the system described and explain how it works.

In the bowl-shaped valley of Chapters 7 and 8 you could also calculate the mechanical advantage of the defense ramp, which was 0.5 miles long and perhaps 100 feet high. Mechanical advantage of an inclined plane equals length divided by height. How much force would it take to replace the boulder on the rim?

Force and Fluid Pressure

Pressure equals force divided by area. Pressure increases as the force increases or the area decreases. You may have discussed air pressure with students or increasing pressure at great depths in the water. On Mesklin hydrogen is the principal atmospheric gas and is much lighter than Earth's air—essentially a mix of nitrogen and oxygen. One of the concerns when Lackland discovers the Mesklinites have to ascend 300 feet is that such a climb would be equivalent to humans climbing to an altitude of 40,000–50,000 feet. (See Chapter 15, "High Ground.") Have students work out the exact figures.

When the Mesklinites are near the equator, Lackland introduces Barlennan to the concept of hollow boats. (The Mesklinites sail lightweight rafts on their methane ocean.) Methane is less than half as dense as water, but still gains considerable density as the party travels north and gravity increases. At some point the Mesklinites' hollow boats fail. Make some assumptions about the materials used to create the boats and have students calculate when boat hulls might be crushed. (See Chapter 14, "The Trouble with Hollow Boats" and Chapter 9, "Over the Edge.")

Light and Optics

Native Mesklinites have no astronomy to speak of and no concept of their world as a spinning ball. Their general impression is that they live at the bottom of a shallow bowl. This illusion results from light refracting as it passes through layers of hydrogen that get progressively more dense closer to the ground—like the mirage illusion we see on Earth when we seem to see water over a hot roadway. In this latter situation, light refracts going from more dense to less dense air and we see a partial reflection of the sky that we interpret as water. Have students diagram the reverse situation on Mesklin. (See Chapter 15, "High Ground.")

Aerodynamics

In Chapter 13, "Slip of the Tongue," Barlennan and crew discover a Mesklinite culture (living close to the equator) that has learned how to make gliders. Could Barlennan steal this technology for use where he lives at higher latitudes? Here's an opportunity to discuss problems of weight versus lift considerations for flying machines. At the end of the book, Barlennan does discover how to make a "lighter-than-hydrogen" machine not unlike Jules Verne's lighter-than-air vehicle on nineteenth-century Earth.

Barlennan's Blackmail Plan

From the beginning, Barlennan has suspected that the Earthmen have one prize he must possess: the knowledge of how to figure out all the amazing things they have shown him are possible. "We want to start at the beginning," Barlennan says, "knowing fully that we cannot learn all you know in our lifetimes. We do hope to learn enough to understand how you have found these things out. . . . If I can start my people learning for themselves, the way you must have—well, I'd be willing to stop selling at a profit."

The Earthmen agree to the bargain. They agree to give Mesklinites the secret of the scientific method of asking questions of nature—the same gift you hope to bestow upon your students.

A Short Fiction Idea: What's Wrong with Giant Ants?

Early sci-fi movies often committed the blunder of creating giant invertebrates to terrorize citizens and confound scientists. Obviously the writers and/or directors were ignorant of—or chose to ignore—the square-cube law: Surface area of enlarged objects increases by the square of the new dimension but volume increases by the cube of that dimension. Thus weight increases faster than the strength of supporting structures and processes like diffusion become less efficient as an organism increases in size. Author Ed Bryant grew up watching such movies and decided to write "giANTS," an SF story that hinged on the correct use of the square-cubed law. In the story, a vicious strain of South American ants, impervious to normal control measures, succumbs to genetic engineering that causes them to grow so large they can no longer function.

You may want to start a discussion of the square-cube law by introducing students to the largest insect on Earth: the African Goliath beetle, with a wingspan greater than a sparrow's. Why don't insects come any bigger? Have the students make a few "artificial insects" out of pipe cleaners and clay. Start by making a series of cardboard boxes. The first can have the dimensions 0.5" × 0.25" × 0.25", the next 1" × 0.5" × 0.5". Keep doubling the linear dimensions up to

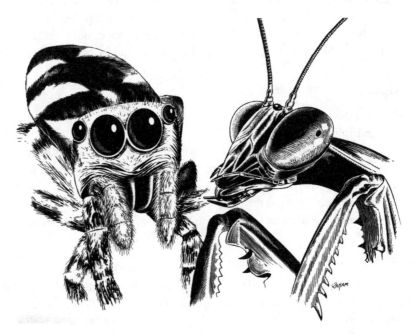

Figure 6.1. Arthropods like the jumping spider (*left*) and praying mantis (*right*) can't be directly scaled up to terrorize us. They would collapse from their own weight.

4" × 2" × 2". Fill each box with modeling clay. These will be the insect bodies. For the first body, make legs out of three pieces of pipe cleaner 1" long. Twist the pipe cleaners together in the middle and bend each projecting "leg" so that you have a freestanding support on which to place the first body. Double pipe cleaner lengths to match subsequent bodies. When do the pipe cleaners fail to support the bodies?

If students then read "giANTS," they should have no problem understanding how scientists defeated the pesky strain of ants. "giANTS" is reprinted in *The Ascent of Wonder* (1994).

BLACK HOLES, QUANTUM UNCERTAINTIES, AND DISTORTED SPACE-TIME

Newton's equations explain physical events in our day-to-day world to perfection. It's no wonder his star shines so brightly in scientific history. Einstein came along and demonstrated that Newton's laws fail to work the same way at speeds approaching that of light and where immense gravity warps the very fabric of space and time. As early as 1783 a Cambridge scholar, John Mitchell, proposed that a sufficiently massive star might collapse upon itself to such an extent that not even light could escape the resulting gravitational field. It wasn't until 1917, however, that the German astronomer Karl Schwartzschild, starting from Einstein's work in general relativity, formulated the precise equations for the radius of such an object, dependent only on its mass. And although American scientist John Wheeler coined the descriptive term "black hole" in 1969 to describe such a "light-eater" (and time-stopper), British physicist Stephen Hawking and his colleague Roger Penrose truly made the term a household word when they proposed that a black hole may have initiated the Big Bang. Refer to Hawking's *A Brief History of Time,* published in 1988, for a readable account.

In 1970, Hawking suggested that black holes were not the ultimate matter disposer after all, but might slowly evaporate over billions of years through the loss of subatomic particles at their surfaces, called event horizons. In 1971 he also proposed that mini black holes, formed at the creation of the universe, might just now—15 billion years later—be undergoing terminal explosive evaporations. Other exotica Hawking has proposed includes wormholes—cylinders of warped space-time that may connect different times and places in the universe. Great stuff for imaginative brain flares among writers of science fiction!

Wellstone and Collapsium

Many writers have used black holes and wormholes as conduits to other times and places so that the real action of a story can occur. But rocket scientist/author Wil McCarthy took several giant steps beyond the obvious and devised a future technology that could rewrite the use of matter to human specifications in truly revolutionary ways. His protagonist in *The Collapsium* (Del Ray, 2000), one Bruno de Towaji, invented a material (collapsium) created by cubical latticeworks of mini black holes the size of protons. Collapsium and another substance, wellstone, revolutionized human existence in "the eighth decade of the Queendom of Sol" like lasers and silicon transistors transformed life in the twentieth century. Wellstone, a silicon latticework laced with carefully controlled impurities, contains electrons in "quantum dots" that can mimic atoms even though they have no nucleus to surround. Wellstone can replicate the properties of traditional elements or, when electrons are replaced by positrons, muons, tau leptons, or other elementary particles, form new and astounding materials (3).

McCarthy's story will entertain you and your students. The eccentric (and vastly wealthy) de Towaji entertains visions of understanding the basic nature of the universe and seeing the very end of time. He carries out his studies on a small planetoid of his own making whose core consists of superdense matter in the form of "neubles" the size of protons—the same building blocks he uses to create stable collapson structures. A rival physicist, Marlon, while trying to create a collapsiter ring about the sun that will speed up interplanetary communications, suffers a setback that could lead to the destruction of the sun itself. Tamra, the beautiful queen of Sol, seeks de Towaji's help. De Towaji and Marlon are professional rivals as well as competitors for Tamra's love, which leads to intrigues and complications on several fronts.

McCarthy also provides appendices, however, which explain the scientific elements of his fiction in some detail. You can effectively use these guides to see if your students really understand the Periodic Table of the Elements and crystal formation, not to mention the nature of matter when it has become squashed to oblivion.

Collapsium and Crystal Structure

De Towaji combines eight massive neubles to make one collapson, a mini black hole weighing some billion tons. He arranges eight collapsons in a basic cubic structure so that adjoining collapsons are a little over 2 cm apart. Are other crystal structures possible? Perhaps. Discuss the six basic crystal structures with students:

1. Regular (cubic): the crystal possesses three mutually perpendicular axes of equal length.
2. Tetragonal: two mutually perpendicular axes of the same length; one shorter or longer.
3. Orthorhombic: three mutually perpendicular axes, all of a different length.
4. Monoclinic: three axes, one pair not perpendicular and all of unequal lengths.
5. Triclinic: three axes, none perpendicular to any other and all of unequal lengths.
6. Hexagonal: three axes of the same length at angles of 60° and in the same plane; a fourth axis of a different length perpendicular to the plane of the other three.

Have students research materials displaying each of these crystal forms, sketch out the collapsium-equivalent structure, and propose a name for each kind of collapsium crystal.

Wellstone and the Periodic Table of the Elements

Perhaps the most effective way to blend the *Collapsium* story into curriculum is during the discussion of the Periodic Table. The miracle substance wellstone, since it can mimic every natural substance, allows you to discuss Mendeleev's grand synthesis and the theory of electron shell organization that helps explain it.

For an excellent treatment of the Periodic Table check out *Conceptual Physical Science,* 2nd edition (1999). The authors show how Mendeleev arrived at his arrangement of the elements, constructing the table first by ordering elements horizontally by atomic number, then by grouping rows (periods) to reflect changes in chemical activity. They demonstrate how periods 1, 2, and 3 have to be shifted so that they align with elements below them with similar properties. They continue by emphasizing the trends that this ordering displays: atomic size generally increasing as you move to the lower left of the table, mirrored by ionization energy increasing as you move toward the upper right of the table; natural groupings of alkali metals, alkali-Earth metals, transition metals, halogens, noble gases, and the block from which semiconductors like silicon reside. They couple this with a discussion of the noble gas shell model of atomic structure, which provides a rationale for electron organization around the nuclei of the elements consistent with observations of chemical activity.

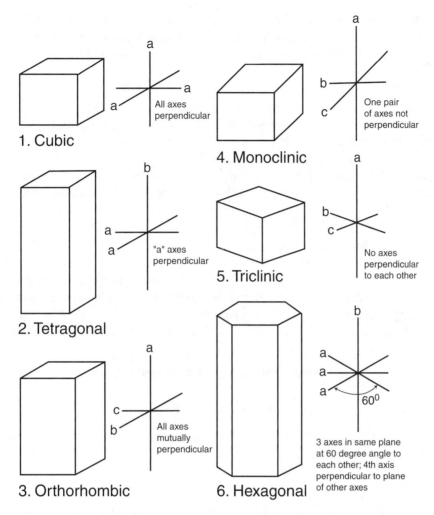

Figure 6.2. A representation of the six basic crystal structures.

Compare "wellstone elements" with their natural counterparts. For example, could you use wellstone iron (which is much less dense than real iron) in the same way the natural substance is used? Why or why not? What substances with entirely unique properties might be formed and why? What other technologies might you need to "tune" your wellstone into different configurations? Without a nucleus, how would wellstone "atoms" vary in size and would this affect how wellstone elements behaved?

Discuss the practice of introducing impurities into semiconductors to improve their application in various aspects of transistor technology.

The abilities of wellstone result from trapping electrons in membranes so thin that their wavelike properties outweigh their particle-like properties. Demonstrate the early experiments that recognized wave/particle duality.

McCarthy mentions that some of the practical uses of wellstone arise as a result of nanotechnology. What is nanotechnology and how might it impact biomedical and other technologies?

The Nature of Black Holes

De Towaji and Marlon play around with potentially very dangerous stuff: superdense matter that warps space and stops time in its tracks. McCarthy mentions that a collapson particle can be destabilized by a wayward muon or other subatomic particle that interacts with it. In addition, time dilation effects change the effective lifetime of otherwise short-lived particles, which causes complications for the collapsitor project. Do any relativistic effects manifest themselves in ways that students can appreciate today?

Show a sample of two prized and attractive metals: gold and silver. The color of silver derives from the fact that this metal absorbs light in the ultraviolet range, but reflects most of the visible light frequencies, resulting in its characteristic silvery-white color. One might expect gold, just below silver in the Periodic Table, to act in a similar way. Scientists puzzled over the color of gold until they realized the role of relativistic effects.

The momentum of particles increases to more than mass times velocity at near-light speeds. The speed of inner-shell electrons for lightweight atoms like silver is modest compared to that of light. Gold atoms are heavy enough that the innermost electrons accelerate to 60% of the speed of light to maintain their orbits. The increased momentum of these inner-shell electrons draws them closer to the nucleus, which effectively increases the shielding effect of that inner shell relative to outer shells, which expand slightly outward. This shifts light absorption characteristics of gold so that some violet and blue light is absorbed. The remaining red/yellow end of the visible spectrum reflects back to our eyes, altering our color perception of a precious metal. Gold's innermost electrons experience only 52 seconds for each of our minutes in Newton's more classical portion of the universe. Sometimes being a little (relativistically) slow can be beautiful.

ADDITIONAL RESOURCES

Science Fiction to Explore

Below I've listed just a sampling of other SF books that you might want to use to discuss classic and/or relativistic physics concepts.

Einstein's Dreams, by Alan Lightman (Pantheon Books, 1993)

This nontraditional novel, marketed as a mainstream title, explores the nature of time by delving into the dreams of a young Albert Einstein when he worked as a patent clerk in Vienna. The book is short and well written without being obscure. The author, fittingly, teaches both physics and writing at MIT. Salman Rushdie said of the book, "It is at once intellectually provocative and touching and comic and so very beautifully written."

Dragon's Egg, by Robert L. Forward (Ballantine Books, 1980)

Robert L. Forward worked as a scientist at the Hughes research labs in California when he wrote this book. Earthmen discover life in a most unlikely place: the surface of a neutron star. Forward manages to make a plausible case for life developing on an object where surface gravity is 67 billion times that of Earth and the magnetic field 2 trillion times stronger. Life there runs on fast time: One Earth hour for the Cheela (the intelligent life form discovered there) equals more than a hundred years of human life. Consequently, Earthmen start out as teachers, but are soon exceeded by their pupils.

Waldo and Magic, Inc., by Robert A. Heinlein (Gregg Press, 1979), earlier printings in 1940, 1942, and 1950. Also, another collection of Heinlein's short works in 1992 by Eric Kotani (*Requiem: New Collected Works*).

The title story, "Waldo," about a crippled inventor who lives in a satellite, gave rise to the term "waldo" to describe any remote-controlled lifting devices that magnify the muscular abilities of their operators. Heinlein wrote juvenile science fiction as well as adult titles and the science is always precisely accurate, reflecting Heinlein's engineering background.

The Fountains of Paradise, by Arthur C. Clarke (Harcourt Brace Jovanovich, 1979)

This book describes two intertwined tales of obsession: King Kalidasa, a second-century monarch of the equatorial island of Taprobane, who sought to reach heaven by creating lofty pleasure gardens, and his twenty-second-century counterpart, Vannevar Morgan, who creates a 36,000-km-high "space elevator" that connects a high mountaintop with a station in geo-synchronous orbit. Excellent story with lots of accurate science to ponder about how such a structure could be created.

Gateway (Ballantine Books, 1977), *Beyond the Blue Event Horizon* (Ballantine Books, 1980), *Heechee Rendezvous* (Ballantine Books, 1984), *The Annals of the Heechee* (Ballantine Books, 1987), and *The Gateway Trip*—a collection of related stories— (Ballantine Books, 1990), by Frederick Pohl

The Heechee lived half a million years ago and spanned the galaxy with their civilization. Then they encountered fierce competitors called the Assassins and were forced to retreat into the relative safety of a black hole. They left behind a cache of autonavigating spacecraft and a blackhole network, subsequently found by humans, that crisscrossed the galaxy. Serious dangers threaten humans as they begin using this network.

A Fire in the Deep (TOR, 1992) and *A Deepness in the Sky* (TOR, 1999), by Vernor Vinge

Both of these stories, set in a far distant future, explore the possibilities for a human trading culture that spans the galaxy and must deal with the relativistic effects of time dilation as they move between different stellar systems. Well-written stories with some dark overtones.

Nano Tech, edited by Jack Dann and Gardner Dozois (Ace books, 1998) (a short-story collection)

This book provides a great collection of short work that deals with aspects of nano technology—the technology of tiny, self-replicating machines operating at the atomic level.

Short Fiction of Note

In "Schwartzchild Radius" (1987) Connie Willis creates a haunting metaphor built around the horrible experiences in the trenches of World War I. Karl Schwartzchild, the German physicist who first calculated the radius at which a collapsed star would no longer emit electromagnetic radiation of any kind, served in the "war to end all wars." "Schwartzchild Radius" was reprinted in the Connie Willis collection *Impossible Things* (Bantam, 1993).

Larry Niven wrote "The Hole Man" (1973) about a mini black hole used as a murder weapon and "planet eater." Poul Anderson wrote "Kyrie" (1969), a love story between a human woman, Eloise, and a sentient, telepathic interstellar "cloud." The cloud saves a human spaceship carrying his beloved, but in the process falls into a black-hole. Because of the nature of black hole boundaries, his final torment will last forever in Eloise's mind. Both these latter stories are reprinted in *The Ascent of Wonder* (TOR, 1994).

Michael Blair, a high school teacher at Theodore Roosevelt High School in Des Moines, Iowa, has created another resource for enterprising high school and middle school teachers called *To Boldly Go . . . Using Star Trek to Teach Physics* (2001). This booklet, partially developed through a grant by the Roy J. Carver Charitable Trust Foundation, will provide many ideas for teaching kinematics, mechanics, wave properties, Newton's laws, relativity, quantum mechanics, and high-energy physics. Contact him at michael.blair@dmps.k12.ia.us or write Michael Blair c/o Des Moines Public Schools, Theodore Roosevelt High School, 4419 Center Street, Des Moines, Iowa 50312.

SF provides vast resources for teaching physical science, but that's only the beginning. We'll explore some fascinating possibilities in the Earth and space sciences in Chapter 7.

NOTES

(1) *Heavy Planet* (see references) contains *Mission of Gravity* as well as a sequel and several related short stories and essays. Clement describes the creation of Mesklin in "Whirligig World," first published in *Astounding Science Fiction* in June 1953.

(2) Clement envisioned Mesklin existing in a star system like 61 Cygni as described in "Whirligig World." (See note 1.)

(3) McCarthy has now written a nonfiction book outlining this idea called *Hacking Matter*. (See Additional Reading.)

REFERENCES

Anderson, Poul. "Kyrie" in David G. Hartwell and Kathryn Cramer, eds. *The Ascent of Wonder: The Evolution of Hard SF*. New York: TOR, 1994, p. 627.

Barlowe, Wayne Douglas, Ian Summers, and Beth Meacham. *Barlowe's Guide to Extraterrestrials*. New York: Workman Publishing, 1979.

Bryant, Edward. "giANT," in David G. Hartwell and Kathryn Cramer, eds. *The Ascent of Wonder: The Evolution of Hard SF*. New York: TOR, 1994.

Clarke, Arthur C. *Fountains of Paradise*. New York: Harcourt Brace Jovanovich, 1979.

Clement, Hal. *Heavy Planet*. New York: Tom Doherty Associates Book, 2002.

Clement, Hal. "Mission of Gravity" in *Astounding Science Fiction* (1954). New York: Pyramid Books (Doubleday), 1962.

Forward, Robert L. *Dragon's Egg*. New York: Del Rey, 1980.

Hawking, Stephen. *A Brief History of Time*. New York: Bantam Books, 1988.

Hartwell, David G., and Kathryn Cramer, eds. *The Ascent of Wonder: The Evolution of Hard SF*. New York: TOR, 1994.

Heinlein, Robert A. "Waldo" in *Waldo and Magic, Inc.* Boston: Gregg Press, 1979, p. 13.

Hewitt, Paul G., John Suchocki, and Leslie A. Hewitt. *Conceptual Physical Science,* 2nd ed. New York: Addison Wesley Longman, Inc., 1999.

Holdstock, Robert, and Malcolm Edwards. *Alien Landscapes*. New York: Mayflower Books, 1979.

Lightman, Alan. *Einstein's Dreams*. New York: Pantheon Books, 1993.

McCarthy, Wil. *The Collapsium*. New York: Del Rey/Ballantine Publishing Group, 2000.

McCarthy, Wil. "Programmable Matter" in *Nature* 407, October 5, 2000: 569.

Niven, Larry. *The Hole Man* (1973) in David G. Hartwell and Kathryn Cramer, eds. *The Ascent of Wonder: The Evolution of Hard SF*. New York: TOR, 1994, p. 474.

Pohl, Frederick. *The Annals of the Heechee*. New York: Del Rey/Ballantine Books, 1987.

Pohl, Frederick. *Beyond the Blue Event Horizon*. New York: Del Rey/Ballantine Books, 1980.

Pohl, Frederick. *Gateway*. New York: Del Rey/Ballantine Books, 1977.

Pohl, Frederick. *Heechee Rendezvous*. New York: Del Rey/Ballantine Books, 1984.

Pohl, Frederick. *Gateway Trip*. New York: Del Rey/Ballantine Books, 1990.

Vinge, Vernor. *A Deepness in the Sky*. New York: TOR (Tom Doherty Associates), 1999.

Vinge, Vernor. *A Fire in the Deep*. New York: TOR (Tom Doherty Associates), 1992.

Willis, Connie. "Schwartzchild Radius" (1987) in *Impossible Things*. New York: Bantam Books, 1993, p. 90.

ADDITIONAL READING

Berlinski, David. *Newton's Gift*. New York: Free Press, 2000.

Clute, John, and Peter Nicholls. *The Encyclopedia of Science Fiction*. New York: St. Martin's Griffin, 1993 (update 1995).

Hawking, Stephen. *A Brief History of Time*. New York: Bantam, 1988.

Hawking, Stephen. *The Universe in a Nutshell*. New York: Bantam, 2001.

McCarthy, Wil. *Hacking Matter: Levitating Chairs, Quantum Mirages, and the Infinite Weirdness of Programmable Atoms*. New York: Basic Books, 2003.

Rees, Martin. *Just Six Numbers*. New York: Basic Books, 2000.

Regis, Ed. *Nano*. New York: Little, Brown, 1995.

CHAPTER 7

SF Resources and Lesson Plans: Earth and Space Sciences

"Then things got crazy. The ground shook. Twigs snapped and bushes started moving. Something made a loud bellow behind us. One majorly big, long-necked, crinkly-skinned 'saur with tree trunk-sized legs came crashing through the underbrush onto the beach. We ran like our butts were on fire."

Neesha Olifee, character in *The Deep Time Diaries,* by Gary Raham

EARTH, LIFE, AND DEEP TIME

One of the most difficult concepts for anyone to grasp is the immensity of geological time. Processes that operate over this gulf of time, like long-term climate change, continental drift, species evolution and extinction, and the birth and death of not only star systems but the universe itself, present concepts equally hard to bend one's mind around. Science fiction may be the only literary form, with the possible exception of some poetry, that utilizes such a vast temporal backdrop for its tales. Sometimes, as in Isaac Asimov's *Foundation* series involving the rise and fall of a galactic empire, stories cover many generations. Other times, as in Heinlein's *Methuselah's Children,* long-lived humans experience "deep time" (a term invented by the writer John McPhee [1]) directly. A third approach, extending back to *The Time Machine,* by H. G. Wells, invokes some form of time travel. I used a method of wormhole time travel in my book *The Deep Time Diaries* to send a twentieth-century family back 800 million years into Earth's past. Science teachers Vicky Jordan, Mark Barnes, and I used this book to teach an interdisciplinary course at Wellington Junior High in northern Colorado.

Explorations with Deep Time Diaries

The Concept

The Deep Time Diaries consists of a sequence of diary entries by ten-year-old Neesha and fourteen-year-old Jon Olifee, siblings who share the usual combination of love and rivalry. The book is illustrated with sketches and full-color art in the style of a naturalist's journal. Factual information at the end of each section provides background, maps, and references for student and teacher. Ms. Jordan and Mr. Barnes saw the potential for using the book to address both Colorado English and science standards for eighth-grade students. The authors believed that, combined with a visit to the Denver Museum of Nature and Science and several author presentations, the unit would broaden students' experience and provide them with inspiration from a writer/ illustrator who lived in their own community. After three years of development, the unit is eagerly awaited by eighth-grade students each year. Several other schools within the district have either adopted the unit or plan to do so.

Science content included information about the age of the Earth, relative versus absolute dat-

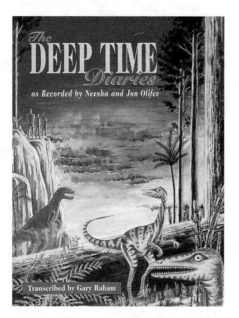

Figure 7.1. *The Deep Time Diaries*, written and illustrated by the author, provides a fictional tale that can serve to explore topics in both the sciences and the arts.

ing techniques, the process of fossilization, the significance of fossils to the study of Earth history and evolution, critical thinking and the scientific method, and rock types and their cycling over time. English assignments addressed various aspects of creative writing including figurative language, the vocabulary of various scientific disciplines, sensory details, punctuation, capitalization, and spelling. Creating the main project of the unit—students' own deep time diaries—also involved sharpening research and speaking skills and learning to make effective PowerPoint presentations. The authors' visits reinforced content in both areas and allowed students to see the creative process exemplified by the authors' personal experience in researching, writing, and illustrating the book.

The Deep Time Diaries Unit

Three figures provide more detailed information about the unit. Figure 7.2 provides an outline for the science evaluation of the journaling activity (items with an asterisk relate directly to Colorado science content standards). Figure 7.3 is a Science rubric and Figure 7.4 shows the eighth-grade English rubric. Refer to Appendix 4 for specific samples of some of the curriculum developed.

Specific Teaching Labs and Activities

Geological Timeline—The History of Life on Earth: Students construct a scale model of the geological timeline using a chart that contains eras, periods, events during each time interval, and the duration of each time interval (in millions of years). They then calculate lengths for time intervals using 1 mm = 1 million years to render their timelines on a roll of adding-machine paper. The student-illustrated timelines grace a hallway outside the classroom. The length of the roll prior to the beginning of the fossil record, not to mention the tiny space left for human habitation of Earth, always astonishes students.

Thundering Flocks of Sauropods: This assignment, adapted from a California Academy of Sciences activity, allows students to analyze an actual sauropod trackway by coloring in the footprint trails of individual dinosaurs and deducing various things, including direction of travel, herding behavior, evidence of predation, and animal size.

Animal Adaptations—Yesterday and Today: Students visit seven lab stations with different fossils, sketch the fossil, and have to answer the following questions: During what geological period did the organism live? What part of the organism's body is this fossil from? How was this structure/body part an adaptation for the organism's survival? What living organism has this kind of adaptation? Write another interesting fact about this ancient organism. Skulls and bones of modern species are provided for comparison so that students can make inferences about the ecological niches of extinct forms.

Radiometric Dating Lab: Students use pennies to demonstrate radioactive decay and graph their results. They dump 100 pennies on the table (representing carbon-14 atoms), record the

---

Science Outline

Science 8: Geology   Name _____

                                         Period _____ Date _____

The Deep Time Diaries

Concept: Earth materials provide clues to its composition, natural processes, and history.

Geological Time

*1. Construct a geological timeline that shows the history of life on Earth.

2. Compare the time period of your life and that of human history to the age of the Earth.

3. Identify and describe at least 3 pieces of scientific evidence that demonstrate the age of the Earth to be over one billion years.

4. Define relative dating and absolute dating and explain what type of information can be learned about deep time from both techniques.

*5. Draw how the position and shape of today's continents have changed through geological time.

Fossils

6. Define fossil.

*7. Describe the following processes by which fossils form, and give an example of each:

| Amber | Petrification | Mummification | Freezing | Carbonization |
| Cast | Mold | Trace fossils | Molecular fossils | |

*8. Model a process of fossilization.

*9. Explain how fossils are evidence that life has changed over time.

*10. List at least 3 organisms that have not changed much since prehistoric times (living fossils) and 3 organisms that have a distinct fossil record of their evolutionary history. Explain what causes some organisms to change while others remain relatively the same.

*11. Compare the teeth or other anatomy of living animals to that of extinct animal fossils, and hypothesize what the diets of the extinct animals may have been.

Figure 7.2. Outline for eighth-grade student unit with Colorado science content items marked with an asterisk.

Science 8: *The Deep Time Diaries*

Science Rubric
Journal Rubric
(The journal will be worth 150 points)

Name:_____

Period:_____Date:_____

Category	X5	X4	X3	X2	X1
Animals (6 points) The journal entries include:	Thorough descriptions and names of 3 appropriate animals written as key parts of the story, with accurate drawings of at least 2 of the animals.	Minimal descriptions and names of 3 appropriate animals with at least 1 drawn. Some descriptions may be "sidebars" or drawings not labeled.	Descriptions and names of 2 or more appropriate animals with a drawing of 1 or more of the animals, or no drawings of the 3 animals.	Descriptions or names of 2 appropriate animals. No drawings.	Description and name of 1 appropriate animal. No drawings.
Plants (6 points) The journal entries include:	Descriptions and names of 3 appropriate plants included as key elements within the story with accurate drawings of at least 2 of the plants.	Descriptions and names of 3 appropriate plants with a drawing of at least 1 plant. Some of the descriptions may be "sidebars" and not part of story.	Descriptions and names of 2 or more appropriate plants with a drawing of at least 1 of the plants, or no drawings of the 3 plants.	Descriptions or names of 2 or more appropriate plants. No drawings.	Descriptions and name of 1 appropriate plant. No drawings.
Continents and environmental conditions (5 points) The journal entries include:	A detailed drawing of the shape and position of the continents and a detailed description of the env. cond. that could be found in that time period.	A drawing of the shape and position of the continents and a description of the env. cond., but lacking detail or not part of the story.	Both parts included, but the shape and position of the continents OR the description of the env. cond. is sloppy, incorrect or incomplete.	A drawing of the shape and position of the continents OR a description of the env. cond. (entries only include one component).	Both the drawing of the shape and position of the continents and the env. cond. are incorrect or incomplete.
Fossilization Process (5 points) The journal entries include:	A detailed example of how an animal or plant can become a fossil, including the overall process of fossilization. Written as part of the story.	An example of how an animal or plant can become a fossil and the process of fossilization, but some details are missing or it is not written as part of the story.	An example of how an animal or plant can become a fossil and the process of fossilization, but some parts are incorrect or incomplete.	A description of the process of fossilization.	An example of the process of fossilization.
Living fossils and extinct organisms (4 points) The journal entries include:	A minimum of 5 examples are included, with 2-3 living fossils and 2-3 extinct organisms. These can be the same plants and animals as above.	A total of 4 examples are included, with 2 living fossils and 2 extinct organisms.	A total of 3 or 4 examples are included, with 1-2 living fossils and 1-2 extinct organisms.	A total of 2-3 examples are included, with 0-3 living fossils and 0-3 extinct organisms OR not labeled.	Less than 2 examples are included, with 0-3 living fossils and 0-3 extinct organisms.
Bibliography (4 points) A separate, last page	Minimum of 4 sources, typed in proper format.	Minimum of 3 sources typed or 4 sources hand written properly OR entries have minor mistakes.	2 or more sources hand written in proper format OR minor mistakes.	Sources not written in proper format or incomplete.	Only one source cited.

Maximum journal score for each difficulty level equals the sum of the maximum possible points in each Category times the point value in the appropriate column. Thus, in the X5 column, Maximum score for "Animals" = 30 + "Plants" = 30 + "Continents etc." = 25 + "Fossilization Process = 25 + "Living Fossils" = 20 + "Bibliography" = 20 for a total of 150 points.

Figure 7.3. Science rubric for *The Deep Time Diaries* unit.

number of pennies tails-up (atoms that have decayed to nitrogen-14), and remove them. They collect the remaining pennies and repeat the procedure until no pennies remain. They calculate the time it takes half their pennies to "decay" (half-life) and graph flip number (time elapsed) versus number of pennies with heads (radioactive atoms remaining). They also answer questions relating to the best use of different radioactive elements for dating various materials.

English 8 Rubric

Writing and Speaking: Write using the following devices: figurative language, vocabulary appropriate to audience and topic, sensory detail (descriptive), different points of view.

Category	5	4	3	2	1
Figurative language (metaphor, simile, personification)	Journal includes 5 examples of figurative language.	Journal includes 4 examples of figurative language.	Journal includes 3 examples of figurative language.	Journal includes 2 examples of figurative language.	Journal includes 1 example of figurative language.
Vocabulary appropriate to audience and topic	Entries name 6 scientific terms for living organisms.	Entries name 5 scientific terms for living organisms.	Entries name 4 scientific terms for living organisms.	Entries name 3 scientific terms for living organisms.	Entries name 2 scientific terms for living organisms.
Sensory details	Entries include 5 sensory details, and journal includes examples of all five senses.	Entries include 4 sensory details, and journal includes examples of all five senses.	Entries include 3 sensory details, and journal includes examples of all five senses.	Entries include 2 sensory details, and journal includes examples of all five senses.	Entries include 1 sensory detail, and journal includes examples of all five senses.

Language Structure: Demonstrate correct punctuation, capitalization, and spelling

Punctuation, capitalization, and spelling	Entries have 1 or fewer mistakes in Punctuation, Capitilization, or Spelling.	Entries have 2 mistakes in Punctuation, Capitilization, or Spelling.	Entries have 3 mistakes in Punctuation, Capitilization, or Spelling.	Entries have 4 mistakes in Punctuation, Capitilization, or Spelling.	Entries have 5 mistakes in Punctuation, Capitilization, or Spelling.

Figure 7.4. English rubric for *The Deep Time Diaries* unit.

Make Your Own Fossil: Students make their own copies of fossils using plaster of paris. They learn the difference between casts, molds, and trace fossils. They also make note of what can and cannot be learned from fossils. A variation: each group of students makes molds and casts (partial or complete) of common "mystery" objects, then exchanges them with another group. Each group must analyze these "future fossils" and deduce what they can from them.

Author/Illustrator-aided Activities

Drawing Dinosaurs: After some warm-up drawing exercises and artist "tricks-of-the-trade," students sketch dinosaur museum-replica plastic models using a strong lighting source that casts dramatic shadows. Students learn what liberties paleoartists can and cannot take when reconstructing the past. I created "Five Commandments" for the paleoartist: (1) Know Your Anatomy (in order to draw a creature that is realistic and scientifically accurate, using the latest findings); (2) Know the Experts (in order to know what the most recent studies reveal); (3) Understand Ecology (so that you can recreate the world in which an organism lived); (4) Know Your Art Well (so that your drawings and paintings look convincing); and (5) Seize the Dramatic Moment (to catch the viewer's full attention).

Yikes! Where Do I Start?: The author/illustrator leads students in creating characters for their fictional diaries (see below). He also provides a chart that shows what-lived-when so that students populate their time periods accurately. The museum visit provides additional information.

A Character-building Résumé: Students learn to build a résumé for their main character(s) by answering questions about the characters' life experience, background, friends, favorite activities, work experience, and unique qualities. They experience the process creative writers go through to create a memorable story.

A Day on the Beach: The author/illustrator invites students to complete a brief writing assignment while he does the same, using characters the students have chosen. Kids become very creative! Here is the setup:

> You are walking along a beach after a storm. Dark, tattered clouds still lurk on the horizon and a few drops of rain poke holes in the wet sand at your feet. As you look down, you see fresh animal tracks paralleling the shoreline. You follow them until they disappear among the jumbled boulders of a rock outcrop. You scramble over the wet rocks and find yourself in a cove. The animal you have been tracking is there, too.

What Happens Next? In a paragraph describe what you find in the cove. The animal should be from the geological era you studied. What do you see, smell, feel, hear, and touch? Try to use at least one metaphor and one simile.

In a second paragraph, describe the same scene, but now you are the animal! Again, what do you see, smell, hear, and touch? Students must stretch their imaginations to see the world through the senses and perceptions of different kinds of creatures. The English teacher promotes the use of engaging metaphors, similes, and sensory-based description for creative writing.

Results, Costs, and Other Resources

One student teacher remarked how pleased she was to be able to see her students perform in areas unfamiliar to her. Mediocre science students sometimes created exceptional writing, or vice versa. Students with artistic abilities could shine in some of the activities. Experienced teachers saw 99% of the students complete the fairly complex diary assignment (2 incompletions out of 160 students). Science teachers addressed nine and English teachers addressed eleven state standards. Students also gained experience with media technology and researching techniques.

In post-unit surveys, several students remarked that it was their favorite science unit and seventh graders, who had heard about the unit, eagerly looked forward to their experience with it in eighth grade.

Vicky Jordan funded the project with local grant money. Book purchases, fees for the author/illustrator visits, and field trip expenses constituted the major costs. Books will last for several years. Author visits can be reduced or eliminated, as could the field trip, but teachers felt both features added considerably to the unit.

Feel free to substitute different books for a similar unit and draw on local talent for author and/or illustrator visits. Other titles that might lend themselves to a geology/Earth history/creative writing unit include *After Man, A Zoology of the Future* by Dougal Dixon, *The Time Machine* by H. G. Wells, *The Dechronization of Sam Magruder* by George Gaylord Simpson, and *Jurassic Park* by Michael Crichton. For tapping sources of regional talent for artists, writers, and scientists, refer to the section entitled "Enticing Experts into the Classroom" in Appendix 1.

SHORT FICTION SET IN DEEP TIME

Dinosaurs punch the wonder buttons of every generation of kids, some of whom grow up to be writers, artists, and scientists. Byron Preiss, an editor of many science titles, and Robert Silverberg, an SF author of repute, teamed up to create a book called *The Ultimate Dinosaur* (Bantam, 1992), which pooled the talents of prominent contributors in each category. Scientists like Peter Dodson, Ken Carpenter, and Phillip J. Currie wrote on matters of science fact while tale-spinners like L. Sprague de Camp, Gregory Benford, and Connie Willis wrote speculations spun from their factual threads. Doug Henderson, Bob Eggleton, and other paleoartists brought the past to life with their images.

In "Unnatural Enemy," for example, Poul Anderson writes about Harpoon, an aging male *Elasmosaurus* who is wounded in a battle with a giant Cretaceous shark. The loss of a flipper causes Harpoon to lose some mobility and he has a harder time nabbing his usual diet of fish. He first goes after shellfish and other fairly tame fare, but learns, with a little cunning and boldness, that he can attack larger prey, including his former tormentor. The reader experiences a Cretaceous world consistent with known facts and based on reasonable assumptions derived from the behavior of modern species in similar ecological niches. Have students read both the factual article and the fiction and make a list of what is based on hard evidence and what is made up. Lead a discussion about why Anderson may have speculated as he did about Harpoon's behavior, giving suitable examples from living species.

Gregory Benford in "Shakers of the Earth" tells of love shared by two paleontologists, both for their work and for each other. They discover the remains of a huge sauropod whose hollow bones have managed to preserve enough unfossilized tissue to provide its DNA composition. Over a lifetime of work they manage to recreate living saurians and they build "Kansas Sauropod Park." Sound familiar? This story was written about the same time as *Jurassic Park*—similar ideas were at large. Have students compare and contrast the methods used to recreate dinosaurs in both stories and speculate on the feasibility of each.

In "Dawn of the Endless Night" Harry Harrison describes the impact of the asteroid that ended the Cretaceous era from the viewpoint of an intelligent race of reptilians (the Yilane) near the dawn of their scientific era. The scientist, Akotolp, eventually realizes her world is coming to an end and ponders the nocturnal mammalian "vermin" who will eventually become their successors as they scurry about in a devastated world.

Other stories that are sure to give you ideas for the classroom include "Besides a Dinosaur, Whatta Ya Wanna Be When You Grow Up" by Ray Bradbury; "The Green Buffalo" by Harry Turtledove; "Herding with the Hadrosaurs" by Michael Bishop; "The Late Cretaceous," by Connie Willis; and "Crocamander Quest," by L. Sprague de Camp.

ALIENS IN DEEP SPACE AND PLANET-BUILDING

SF writers may seem "free and easy" when they create strange worlds and bizarre aliens, but the good ones spend a lot of time world- and alien-building using sound scientific knowledge and principles. This exercise requires broad knowledge of many scientific disciplines—just the ticket for challenging your students and introducing a variety of scientific principles. I invite you to engage your students in this process. They will love it!

Imagine an Alien . . .

Begin by having students create an alien creature. They can start by drawing a picture, but they must also provide some specific information:

- What is the height and weight of an adult?
- What is its body composed of and how is it structured?
- How does it move around?
- How does it get and use energy?
- What kind of sensory organs does it have?

- How long does it live?

- How does it reproduce? What is its life cycle?

For comparison, you will need to have students compile similar information about human beings as a point of reference and you may also want to point out variations in some different Earth animals and plants that might seem pretty alien even though all of them come from the same planet and use the same biochemical pathways. For a human being:

Adult height and weight (of a male): 2 meters, 68 kg.

Body composition and structure: Tissues composed primarily of carbon, hydrogen, oxygen, and nitrogen layered on a hard, calcium-phosphate framework (skeleton).

Locomotion: Walks or runs upright on two legs.

Physiology: Eats carbon compounds, burns them with inhaled oxygen, exhales carbon dioxide, excretes solids and ammonia compounds. Maintains constant body temperature. Requires liquid water.

Sensory organs: Senses light (with eyes), sound (with ears), chemical stimulae (taste and smell), and texture (through touch).

Average life span: 35 years (in the "wild"), 75 years (in "civilized" societies).

Reproduction/life cycle: Two sexes that produce 1–6 offspring. Social. Parental/group care until sexual maturity.

Even just listing these basic facts (with appropriate explanation) may provide some perspective on the human animal many students may not have considered recently. Add to this a discussion about insects and other animals with an external skeleton and creatures with different sensory ranges and specialties, animals and plants with an alternation of generations or some sort of metamorphosis, and you can quickly expand the options explored on our own small planet. Mention microbes that "burn" sulfur compounds or live in hot springs, within rocks, and in other exotic habitats, and the variety gets richer.

For a look at how science fiction illustrators have recreated classic aliens and their worlds, refer to Barlowe et al., *Barlowe's Guide to Extraterrestrials* and Holdstock and Edwards, *Alien Landscapes.*

In a different approach to alien-making, Catherine Matthews in *Science Scope* magazine shows how to teach some genetics to seventh graders. Students define a series of a dozen alien traits (body shape, head shape, legs, wings/tail, eyes on stalks, mouth, color, hair, suction cups, nose, ears, and gender) and determine whether various alleles for these traits are dominant, recessive, or incompletely dominant. They create a trait key for each individual, then write a tasteful "personals ad" to shop for a mate. (For example, they may want children with wings and a triangular head, so they would look for those features.) To determine the genotypes of their children they have to make a set of twelve Punnett squares to determine the possible variations in traits. They end up drawing their babies with some artistic variations on the basic traits. Triangular heads could vary, for instance, in angle size and sharpness of vertices. The article provides complete details on setting up the exercise.

. . . Build His (Her, or Its) World

Once students have created an alien that appeals to them, their job is to construct a *plausible* world on which this creature could have evolved. Determining this plausibility will lead them to many topics, including star and planet composition and formation, the mechanics of planetary systems, organic and inorganic chemistry, changing weather and climate, as well as exercising math skills in computation and graphing. Students need to determine:

- Characteristics of the alien's home solar system

  The spectral class of the star

  The star's temperature and mass

- Characteristics of the alien's home planet

  Distance from its sun and orbital period

  Day length (rotational period) and axial tilt

  Diameter, mass, density, and surface gravity (relative to Earth)

  Atmospheric composition

  Current age

  Average temperature and general arrangement of oceans, land, and weather patterns

Let's look at some of the information you will want to impart to give students the tools they will need to determine these things.

Once Around a Star . . .

First you will want to explain the process of star formation—how stars (and their attendant planets) condense from interstellar gas and how the color, brightness, and size of stars depend on the amount of starting material available and the age of the star. The H-R (Hertsprung-Russell) diagram (Fig. 7.5) provides the best summary of this information. You can trace a young star from its formative red giant phase, through its Main Sequence middle age, to its red supergiant old age, and its ultimate degeneration to a cinder, neutron star, or black hole.

Next, you will need to show that some stars are bad choices for an intelligent race's home sun. Population I stars (those formed first in the history of the universe and composed almost entirely of hydrogen and helium) won't produce planets that have a rich enough medley of elements to support life. Population I stars "cook" many more elements within their interiors as they contract and age (after most of the hydrogen has fused to helium), but these heavier elements are only added back to the interstellar medium when a star blows off its outer layers as a nova or explodes as a supernova. Population II stars, like our sun and its planets, condensed from this enriched stew of elements.

Stars also need a long, stable middle age to allow time enough for life to evolve on their planets. Blue giants, for example, burn out within a few million to a couple of billion years—not enough time for complex life to evolve, based on what we know of our own evolution. Red dwarfs may survive for ten billion years, but their furnaces burn at low temperatures. Planets would have to circle close to the star to form in the life-friendly zone where water can exist as a liquid, at least part of the time, but if planets are too close to their sun they will be ripped apart by gravitational forces. Thus we have a "Goldilocks" problem. Stars can't be too hot (and burn up fast) or too cold. They have to fall within a range that gives their planets adequate heat and ten billion years or so to incubate some precocious life forms. Our sun is classed as a G2 (yellow) star with an average temperature of 5770°K and an expected life span of ten billion years. Students would be

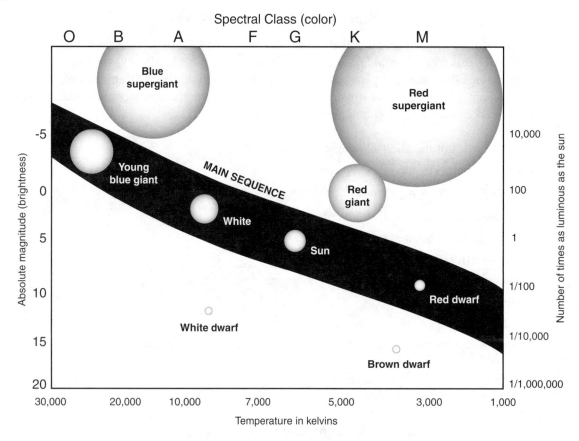

Figure 7.5. The Hertsprung-Russell diagram provides a guide for selecting a star system capable of supporting life.

wise to select a star with spectral classes between F5 and K5 (each spectral class has ten subdivisions), although some SF writers get creative with other solutions. Robert L. Forward wrote a convincing book (*Dragon's Egg,* 1980) about very fast-evolving life forms that developed on the *surface* of a neutron star!

. . . There Was a Beautiful Planet

The Earth provides the points of reference to select other potential intelligent-life-bearing planets, just as humans provide a reference point for creating aliens. This doesn't mean that students need to select strictly Earth-like planets—there are other interesting options—but they should know Earth's "stats:" 149.6 million km from the sun, orbital period of 365.25 days, rotational period of 23 hours, 56 minutes, diameter of 12,756 km at the equator, density of 5.4, nitrogen/oxygen atmosphere, average temperature of 22°C, and current age of 4.6 billion years. Its crustal surface, divided into a number of fragmented "plates," floats on a mantel kept fluid with the heat from a nickel-iron core. Mountains rise and fall, long-term weather patterns shift from time to time, but water can exist in all three phases: gas, liquid, and solid.

Earth's solar system provides examples of other kinds of planets (and their moons) that might harbor life. Presumably other stars would produce a similar range of planetary types. Stanley Schmidt in *Aliens and Alien Societies* summarizes them as follows:

Superjovians: Masses several times that of Jupiter, coming close to becoming a small star in their own right. If they didn't harbor life on their surfaces, some of their moons could support

Earth-like conditions. Hal Clement's *Mission of Gravity* (see Chapter 6) deals with life forms adapted to the immense gravity (and gravitational extremes from equator to pole) on such a planet (Mesklin).

Jovians: Jupiter-like planets with methane-ammonia atmospheres and a nonrocky core.

Subjovians: Planets like Uranus or Neptune with less mass than Jupiter and less hydrogen and helium in their atmospheres.

Superterrestrials: Rocky-cored planets with perhaps eight times the Earth's mass and a similar density. Such planets would have up to twice Earth's diameter and surface gravity.

Terrestrials: Planets with a similar composition to Earth, but may vary in their distance from a star. Earth and Venus are nearly identical "twins" in terms of size and composition, but their distance from the sun has produced very different atmospheres and surface temperatures.

Subterrestrials: Rocky planets smaller than the Earth, like Mercury, Mars, and the Earth's moon. Their distance from the sun and their status as independent planet or satellite affect surface conditions. They are less capable of holding an atmosphere than Earth.

Other valuable references for proper "world-building" include Stephen L. Gillett's *World-Building, Writer's Guide to Constructing Star Systems and Life-supporting Planets* and Amit Goswami's *The Cosmic Dancers: Exploring the Physics of Science Fiction*. An appendix in the latter book contains some useful equations for determining some basic features of your planet. Refer also to Chapter 8 in this book in the section titled "Terraforming Arrakis and Other Planets" for ways alien planets could be made more Earth-like.

As in the *Deep Time Diaries* project described earlier, this project lends itself to use by other teachers in your school. English teachers can have students write a short story based on their alien and planet-building research. Art teachers can encourage visual representations of "Planet X" and its inhabitants. Math teachers can supervise physics calculations along with any necessary tables and graphs. And, when creatively executed, students won't even realize that entertaining fiction has been hijacked in the cause of education!

NOTE

(1) Beginning in 1981, John McPhee wrote eloquently on geology in a series of books, including *Basin and Range* and *Rising from the Plains*. The book *Annals of the Former World* (see Additional Reading), compiles his geological writings (including the two books mentioned above) over a twenty-year period.

REFERENCES

Anderson, Poul. "Unnatural Enemy" in *The Ultimate Dinosaur*. New York: Bantam/Byron Preiss, 1992, p. 244.

Barlowe, Wayne Douglas, Ian Summers, and Beth Meacham. *Barlowe's Guide to Extraterrestrials*. New York: Workman Publishing, 1979.

Benford, Gregory. "Shakers of the Earth" in *The Ultimate Dinosaur*. New York: Bantam/Byron Preiss, 1992, p. 112.

Bishop, Michael. "Herding with the Hadrosaurs" in *The Ultimate Dinosaur*. New York: Bantam/Byron Preiss, 1992, p. 196.

Bradbury, Ray. "Besides a Dinosaur, Whatta Ya Wanna Be When You Grow Up" in *The Ultimate Dinosaur*. New York: Bantam/Byron Preiss, 1992, p. 220.

Clement, Hal. *Mission of Gravity* (1953). New York: Pyramid Books (Doubleday), 1962.

Crichton, Michael. *Jurassic Park*. New York: Alfred A. Knopf, 1991.

de Camp, L. Sprague. "Crocamander Quest" in *The Ultimate Dinosaur*. New York: Bantam/Byron Preiss, 1992, p. 10.

Forward, Robert L. *Dragon's Egg*. New York: Del Rey, 1980.

Gillett, Stephen L. *World-Building, a Writer's Guide to Constructing Star Systems and Life-supporting Planets*. Cincinnati, OH: Writers' Digest Books, 1996.

Goswami, Amit. *The Cosmic Dancers: Exploring the Physics of Science Fiction*. New York: Harper & Row, 1983.

Harrison, Harry. "Dawn of the Endless Night" in *The Ultimate Dinosaur*. New York: Bantam/Byron Preiss, 1992, p. 264.

Holdstock, Robert, and Malcolm Edwards. *Alien Landscapes*. New York: Mayflower Books, 1979.

Mathews, Catherine. "The Alien Lab: A Study in Genetics" in *Science Scope* 26, no. 2, October 2002.

Preiss, Byron, and Robert Silverberg, eds. *The Ultimate Dinosaur*. New York: Bantam Books, 1992.

Raham, R. Gary. *The Deep Time Diaries*. Golden, CO: Fulcrum Publishing, 2000.

Schmidt, Stanley. *Aliens and Alien Societies*. Cincinnati, OH: Writers' Digest Books, 1995.

Simpson, George Gaylord. *The Dechronization of Sam Magruder*. New York: St. Martin's Press, 1996.

Turtledove, Harry. "The Green Buffalo" in *The Ultimate Dinosaur*. New York: Bantam/Byron Preiss, 1992, p. 306.

Willis, Connie. "The Late Cretaceous" in *The Ultimate Dinosaur*. New York: Bantam/Byron Preiss, 1992, p. 156.

ADDITIONAL READING

Dixon, Dougal. *After Man: A Zoology of the Future*. New York: St. Martin's Press, 1981.

Dixon, Dougal. *Man after Man: An Anthropology of the Future*. New York: St. Martin's Press, 1990.

Dixon, Dougal, and John Adams. *The Future Is Wild*. Toronto, Ontario: Firefly Books, 2003.

McPhee, John. *Annals of the Former World*. New York: Farrar, Straus & Giroux, 1998.

CHAPTER 8

SF Resources and Lesson Plans: The Life Sciences

"There's an internally recognized beauty of motion and balance on any man-healthy planet. You see in this beauty a dynamic stabilizing effect essential to all life. Its aim is simple: to maintain and produce coordinated patterns of greater and greater diversity. Life improves the closed system's capacity to sustain life. Life—all life—is in the service of life."
Pardot Kynes, First Planetologist of Arrakis as quoted by Frank Herbert, *Dune*

Horrific monsters usually inhabit the pages of bad science fiction. These creatures exist as cardboard enemies intent on the destruction of our heroic character or perhaps all of humankind. Sometimes they have inexplicable desires for human females and carry them off to await rescue by incensed human males. Monsters may inhabit the pages of good science fiction, too, with the difference being that their author/creators have given them a history, biological and personal, that reveals why they appear monstrous to human protagonists.

Effective authors expend great time and energy creating believable worlds for their characters. The works they have produced provide excellent opportunities to allow students to imagine what an entire global ecology might look like that evolved elsewhere (or elsewhen) in the universe. Frank Herbert helped pioneer this approach to science fiction with *Dune* (1965). I'll provide suggestions for using the biota of Arrakis and other fictional planets to help students think more deeply about biology on our own near-and-dear Earth.

Everyone loves those clever automatons that mimic human thought and action. Sometimes they're called robots, sometimes androids, and sometimes just artificial intelligences. Sometimes they are man/machine hybrids. I will suggest ways to put some of the most popular fictional examples of these creatures "on trial" to explore what it means to be alive, sentient, and human.

And where is ET, anyway? Why have we seen no verifiable evidence of extraterrestrial life after many years of looking? (See Chapter 4, note 5, regarding the Fermi paradox.) The Drake Equation allows students to examine all the factors that contribute to the evolution of life and especially technological civilizations capable of communicating with each other.

OF SPICE AND SANDWORMS

Arrakis

Frank Herbert conceived the planet Arrakis, central to his novel *Dune,* in intricate detail. As mentioned in Chapter 4, he has been credited with raising the entire concept of ecology to consciousness within popular culture (1). While my intent is to show biology teachers how they might use *Dune* in conjunction with a unit on ecology, the tale also includes much political intrigue, the development of psychic powers, and the rise of a religion built around the Messiah-like Paul Atreides—themes that might suit other areas of study as well.

Arrakis circles the star Canopus. Desert stretches unbroken between latitudes 60°N and 70°S. Although there is past evidence of surface water, most of what remains lies trapped in two small polar caps and beneath the surface of the planet. Humans colonized two urban centers in the Imperial and Hagga Basins: Arrakeen and Carthag. Imperial subjects live in villages near these cities. Nomadic clans called Fremen have managed to colonize some of the open desert habitats through scrupulous management of water, building elaborate cave systems for living and supply areas, and harnessing the enormous, indigenous sandworms for transportation. The sandworms are also the source of Arrakis' only export: melange (also referred to as spice). This substance, a by-product of the sandworm's life cycle, can extend human life and promote visions.

Sandworm Biology

Adult sandworms, also known as Shai-Hulud, may be 200 to 400 meters long and burrow through the sands like roving earthquakes. They start life as small planktonic forms living in the sand and are consumed as food by adults. Survivors develop into the half-plant–half-animal form called Little Makers or sand trout. A few centimeters on a side, the roughly diamond-shaped, leathery sand trout swim mostly in deep sand using rows of cilia along the sides of their bodies. They can link together with these cilia and form living sacks that surround pockets of water, which are poisonous to adult sandworms. Water, mixed with sand trout excretions, becomes a prespice mass when fermented by a fungus. A carbon dioxide bubble formed during the process "blows" the prespice mass to the surface (destroying millions of sand trout in the process) where, with the action of sunlight, it becomes melange. Melange serves as food for sand plankton. Surviving sand trout enter an encysted hibernation stage and emerge as adult sandworms in six years.

Sandworms usually travel beneath the surface of the sand, but Fremen have learned they can keep sandworms above surface and ride them if they hook the front edge of a ring segment and hold it open. The sandworm doesn't like getting sand into its sensitive interior through the openings thus produced. Sandworms can be attracted by any surface vibration. When Fremen wish to summon the creatures intentionally, they use devices called thumpers, which beat in a regular pattern on the sand.

Activities

- Have students draw their interpretation of sandworms, sand plankton, and sand trout and then illustrate the life cycle.

- Compare and contrast sandworm biology with the life cycles of Earth's creatures. For example: Aquatic annelids and mollusks produce very similar, ciliated trochophore larvae that live among the plankton in Earth's oceans. In mollusks the trochophore larvae continue to develop into velliger larvae. Horseshoe crabs also have immature forms that live as part of the plankton.

- No mention is made of sandworm sexuality, but you might have students speculate about how the sand plankton are formed based on what they know of annelid biology on Earth (like the earthworm's hemaphroditic system). Two 400-meter sandworms swapping gametes could make for exciting viewing!

Stillsuits

Because an exposed human can lose up to five liters of water per day on the deserts of Arrakis, Fremen have perfected the stillsuit: an external covering that recycles water efficiently. The stillsuit is a layered garment with the innermost layer porous to allow perspiration to travel through it to two additional outer layers that precipitate salt. Reclaimed water circulates to receptacles called "catch-pockets" through bodily motions and osmosis. The wearer can suck water from these reservoirs through a tube. Thigh pads process waste materials and nose and mouth filters prevent water loss during breathing. An operational stillsuit can restrict water loss to a couple of centiliters per day, mostly through the skin of the hands when they are not covered by gloves. Stilltents provide the same services to travelers who must spend the night in the desert.

Activities

- Have students sketch their version of stillsuits and/or stilltents.

- Have students research the adaptations of animals and plants that live in desert habitats on Earth. Based on their studies, let them suggest other devices the Fremen might have invented.

- Water is so precious on Arrakis that many words and phrases relate to it. For example, Fremen say "Get his water" as a euphemism for killing someone, as water is recaptured from the dead. This is analogous to the many words created in Eskimo culture to describe snow in all its varied forms. Let students create a "phrase book" of other common Fremen sayings. Examples: "His water is most foul" or "His honor is porous" could be an insult. "She would share her last drop" could affirm a person's charity, etc.

Terraforming Arrakis and Other Planets

Appendix I at the end of *Dune* describes Pardot Kynes, a government scientist who convinced the Fremen that Arrakis could be transformed within 400 years into a much more Earth-like planet through a rigorous and sequential planting strategy. Such techniques for making alien planets livable are referred to as "terraforming." Various Earth scientists have suggested ways our planetary neighbor, Mars, might be terraformed. Have students research these ideas and compare them with Pardot Kynes' plans.

As noted in Chapter 3, science fiction writer Kim Stanley Robinson created a classic trilogy about terraforming Mars and Pamela Sargent wrote an epic-style trilogy about the terraforming of Venus. Interested students may want to explore these writers' works.

James Blish, long before the modern era of genetic engineering, wrote a series of short stories that speculated that terraforming alien planets might be much more expensive than changing humanity to fit the world. "Surface Tension," often anthologized, tells the story of humans who are re-engineered to live at microscopic size among protozoan-sized creatures. An expedition ultimately visits "outer space"—the universe beyond the water's surface. You can find "Surface Tension" reprinted in *The Ascent of Wonder* (1994). Blish's "pantropy" stories were also collected as *The Seedling Stars* (1957).

The Ecology of Helliconia

I must also mention another science fiction series that would provide an excellent springboard not only to planetary ecology but to Earth science topics related to long-term climate changes on planets. British author Brian Aldiss wrote *Helliconia Spring* (1982), *Helliconia Summer* (1983), and *Helliconia Winter* (1985). Helliconia is an inhabited planet of a double-star system with an eccentric orbit that provides not only for typical seasons, but for eons-long changes in climate that profoundly affect the life of its inhabitants. The long tableau of events is witnessed by a weary Terran civilization that has placed an observation platform in orbit around Helliconia.

ARTIFICIAL LIFE ON TRIAL

The Tradition of Humaniform Creatures

Artificial life that is not quite human regularly inhabits the pages of horror and science fiction tales. Artificial people first began appearing toward the beginning of the nineteenth century and were conceived as blasphemous and diabolically inspired creatures. As noted in Chapter 2, Mary Shelley at the tender age of nineteen created Dr. Frankenstein's monster, the quintessential artificial man to which all others are compared. Shelley's scientist "reanimated" lifeless tissue with electricity. Subsequent writers envisioned artificial people built completely from raw materials. Karel Capek, in the 1921 play *R.U.R.,* coined the term "robot" from the Czech word "robota" (meaning statute labor) to describe his artificial humans of organic origin—creatures we would today refer to as androids. The term "robot" is now usually reserved for strictly mechanical devices like R2-D2 (2) and C3PO in *Star Wars.* The term "cyborg" describes man/machine hybrids like the infamous Borg in *Star Trek: The Next Generation.* The term "A.I." (for artificial intelligence) may describe any sentient, but not necessarily humaniform, artificial entity such as HAL in *2001: A Space Odyssey* (1968) or Mike in Robert Heinlein's *The Moon Is a Harsh Mistress* (1966).

In the literature of science fiction, the prolific Isaac Asimov carved out a large robotic niche for himself. In the introduction to one of his books, *The Rest of the Robots* (1964), Asimov says that he wanted to rid robots of the Faustian baggage they always seemed to carry that required that they destroy their makers. Every new technology has its safeguards, after all. With the editor John W. Campbell, he formulated the three laws of robotics built into every positronic brain created by General Robotics, Inc.:

First Law: A robot may not injure a human being or, through inaction, allow a human being to come to harm.

Second Law: A robot must obey the orders given it by human beings except where such orders would conflict with the First Law.

Third Law: A robot must protect its own existence as long as such protection does not conflict with the First or Second Law.

Laws, of course, are subject to interpretation, and many of Asimov's robot stories hinged on unusual events that distorted the intent of the three laws. Robot confusion dealing with humans also provides opportunities for humor, as robots like the "droids" in *Star Wars* amply demonstrate.

Because robots and their kin provide such great opportunities for both laughing at ourselves and pondering what it means to be human, they warrant some special attention in the classroom. I propose that putting their favorite artificial creature on trial for the "crime" of being human will offer students many insights into the nature of life, intelligence, and self-awareness.

Setting Up the Courtroom

First, select which artificial creature to put on trial. I will make several suggestions, but you can certainly choose whichever entity is popular at the moment. Then, formulate the charges. For example: "_____, you are accused of being human: of having the qualities or attributes of a human being. If found 'guilty' of such charges, you will be awarded all the rights and responsibilities of human beings. If found innocent, you will be considered mere property of the human beings who own or have created you."

Some students will comprise a panel of jurors. They will vote on the creature's guilt or innocence and must write a position paper that explains their vote, based on the evidence provided. Remaining students will support the offense or defense. You can appoint, or students can elect, a head lawyer or spokesperson for each side. They must question the "witnesses," who will be students who will assume the identity of key individuals (writers, philosophers, religious figures, etc.) who might argue the case in a particular way. The remaining students will be responsible for providing research for the various positions.

In the classroom you can discuss what might fall under the "rights and responsibilities" of being human: the rights to vote, to self-determination, to marry and have progeny, and to own property; the responsibility to obey laws and respect the rights of others. You should also address what it means to be human. Humans are alive and self-aware beings. They feel and often act upon emotions. They are aware of past, present, and future, and the fact of their own eventual death. They are social creatures with a sense of right and wrong. Many believe they have free will and a soul as something distinctive from "mind."

Are artificial intelligences even alive, in the biological sense? Clifford Grobstein in *The Strategy of Life* (1965) attempts to look at Earth from the perspective of an impartial, observing entity. He concludes that life demonstrates the following characteristics:

- It is composed of large molecules (macromolecular).

- It is self-organized in several layers of complexity. Think of cell, tissue, organ, individual, population, community, biome, and perhaps the concept of Gaia as ascending levels of organization.

- It is capable of reproducing itself.

- It is able to capture and process energy and materials in a continuous flow that allows for repairing and rebuilding its various systems.

- It suffers occasional spontaneous changes in the properties of its complexes that allow for increased adaptation and survival.

After discussing the variety of life on Earth and looking at organisms on the borderline (like viruses), students will be in a better position to evaluate their chosen A.I.

Fictional Artificial Intelligences

Below are a few creatures in the literature or movies that could be put on trial.

Commander Data

Data, serving as an officer on board the starship *Enterprise* in *Star Trek: The Next Generation,* pays homage to Asimov's robots as he possesses a positronic brain. In the series we discover that Data is one of two android-style robots invented by the reclusive genius Dr. Sung. Data has no emotions and, like Pinnochio, aspires to becoming more human. Even though he attended the Federation Academy and graduated into the service, he is put on trial in the episode entitled "The Measure of a Man" (1989) as being simply a machine and the property of the Federation. (A Captain Maddox was granted permission to disassemble Data with the hopes of making more androids, but when he couldn't guarantee success in putting Data back together again, Data resigned his commission rather than disobey a direct order. Maddox pursued the issue anyway, bringing charges against Data.) Check www.startrek.com, go to "library" and follow the links to *The Next Generation* episodes, second season, for a summary.

Asimov Robots

In the lead story of Asimov's *I, Robot* (1950) nursemaid robot Robbie runs afoul of a mother jealous of the robot's popularity with her daughter and worried about "what the neighbors will think." This could be a good resource for a younger group of students, because Robbie's young charge is eight years old, and they will be amused that the story is set in the far future of 1998.

In the story "Liar" in the same book, robot Herbie somehow acquired the ability to read people's thoughts during a seemingly standard production run. Here we see how a robot runs afoul of Asimov's First Law by trying to "not bring harm" to the humans around him.

Asimov's quintessential robot, however—who would have to be described as an android—is R. Daniel Olivaw. He first makes an appearance as the assistant to Detective Elijah Baley in *The Naked Sun* (1957). Elijah, an Earthman harboring an inherent distrust of robots, must partner with Olivaw to solve an apparently "impossible" murder on Solaria, a planet where robots greatly outnumber and serve a small number of humans. Olivaw is later woven into Asimov's Foundation series, which takes place in a far distant future and doesn't contain any robots in the original three books. Asimov made Olivaw and other robots unseen players in this future attempting to obey the Three Laws to the limit by keeping the human race from destroying itself. Refer to *The Robots of Dawn* (1983) and *Robots and Empire* (1985).

A.I.'s

Arthur C. Clarke created HAL, an acronym short for Heuristically programmed ALgorithmic computer, to run the ship *Discovery* on its mission to Jupiter to discover something about the mysterious origins of the lunar monolith that had been monitoring the development of humanity for some three million years (Clarke, 1968). HAL easily passes the Turing test for artificial intelligence. British mathematician Alan Turing in the 1940s proposed a practical test for determining whether a machine was intelligent: if you could not distinguish a conversation with said machine from that with a fellow human, the machine must be intelligent. HAL also suffers a mental breakdown, which provides for lots of dramatic tension in the movie, and provides another parallel to human intelligence. But is HAL "human"? See whether your students can decide.

Robert Heinlein's "Mike," in *The Moon Is a Harsh Mistress* (1968), is not the fastest computer on record, but has somehow passed a critical threshold of complexity that pushed him into sentience. Heinlein entertainingly describes the circumstances in Book I, "That Dinkum Thinkum." Mike turns out to be a key element in an American-style revolution by the moon's citizens.

Philip K. Dick's Androids

Philip K. Dick's *Do Androids Dream of Electric Sheep?* (1968) was eventually made into the film *Blade Runner* (1982). In a future with a depleted ecology, the protagonist hunts down androids illegally imported from Mars. In the process, he discovers that society's new Messiah may also be artificial. Dick, an excellent writer, may pursue darker or more adult themes than you wish to deal with. As with all the suggestions here, sample the material first to see how you might adapt a given writer's work.

Witnesses Called for Testimony

Have fun with the witnesses called for prosecution or defense. Pick historical figures and/or contemporary personalities who might have an opinion on such matters. A few suggestions follow.

Philosophers: Aristotle, Immanuel Kant, Friedrich Nietzsche, Ghandi.

Religious figures: Jesus, Mohammed, Buddha, the Pope, the Dalai Lama, Pat Robertson, Mother Teresa.

Scientists: Alan Turing, Marvin Minsky, Carl Sagan, Stephen Hawking, Albert Einstein, Lynn Margulis.

Politicians: Thomas Jefferson, Abraham Lincoln, Theodore or Eleanor Roosevelt, John F. Kennedy, Shirley Temple Black, or the current "star" in the news.

Media personalities: Think in terms of people or characters various actors portray that students are talking about at the moment.

Cartoon characters: Bart Simpson, Bugs Bunny.

Whichever witnesses are called, students must be able to document opinions with research. They will learn much in the process.

IN SEARCH OF ET

First Contact

Tales about meeting alien species provide some of the most engaging stories in science fiction. They are called "First Contact" stories and deal with the impact of the interaction of two alien societies exposed to each other for the first time. One civilization is virtually certain to be older, and more advanced than the other, based on the vast stretches of time over which planets age and provide homes for living creatures. Contact between civilizations on Earth has often been disastrous for the more primitive culture. Since our technological civilization is only a few hundred years old, we would likely be the junior member in any such meeting in the near future. We would be wise to consider the possibilities. After considering some fictional accounts of First Contact, students will be in a position to appreciate an equation that attempts to estimate just how likely we are to encounter an extraterrestrial (ET).

Since the SF literature is vast in this area, I will point out a few suggestions and let you follow threads that seem of interest or authors who tend to create First Contact stories. One early story, simply entitled "First Contact," was written by Murry Leinster in 1945. It was anthologized in softcover in *Contact* (1963). An Earthman discovers that he can communicate with an alien by swapping the equivalent of dirty stories. An anthology edited by Damon Knight called *First Contact* (1971) provides another collection of these tales.

The Mote in God's Eye (1974) by Larry Niven and Jerry Pournelle describes a meeting between humans and another race of equal or superior technology and with similar gifts of treachery and cunning. When the emissaries from the alien species are inadvertently killed, humans must find the alien homeworld and stave off retribution.

Orson Scott Card's protagonist in *Ender's Game* (1984) is a boy, Ender Wiggins, who is recruited at a young age to participate in "war games" that turn out to be real encounters with a ruthless, insect-like species called the buggers. Wiggins is so successful that when he finds out the games have caused near genocide among the buggers, he must deal with the guilt from his role in the operation. In a sequel, *The Speaker for the Dead* (1986), Wiggins makes contact with a very different alien race called the "piggies."

Carl Sagan wrote a well-received book called *Contact* (1985) where aliens communicate by encoding information within the number pi. David Zindell works out a convincing mathematical communication scheme to converse with a god-like entity in *Neverness* (1988).

Jack McDevitt, a newer name in the SF pantheon, has written several titles addressing First Contact issues. Look up *The Hercules Text* (1986), *Infinity Beach* (2000), and *Chindi* (2002). His sparsely populated universe portrayed in the last two titles reflects a current suspicion by astronomers that we should have heard from ET by now.

The Drake Equation

In spite of UFO stories and a cadre of avid believers, and after decades of listening for radio signals from other intelligent species, scientists have discovered no evidence of other intelligent life in the universe. Why? Are other races too far away? Do they not wish to communicate? Are they using means other than radio signals? Or are we alone at this time and place in the universe? Astronomer Frank Drake in the early sixties developed a quantitative formula to try to generate some reasonable estimates for the number of other civilizations in our galaxy that might be trying to communicate with us. Finding numbers for the factors in his equation involves examining subjects ranging from stellar and planetary astronomy to organic chemistry, evolutionary biology, history, politics—even psychology. Allow students to ferret out their own solutions to the equation and you will provide them with a great opportunity for interdisciplinary studies that highlight our own vulnerabilities as a species.

Carl Sagan discusses the Drake equation in some detail in *Cosmos* (1980). His book *Murmurs of Earth* (1978) (some of which was written by Frank Drake) also discusses the problems of trying to communicate with another species that scientists considered when they created the messages affixed to the two *Voyager* spacecraft launched in 1977. The Drake equation can be written as follows:

$$N = N_* f_p n_e f_l f_i f_c f_L$$

N is the number of technical civilizations in our galaxy capable of sending a message by radio waves. The remaining factors in the equation and some of the guesstimates suggested by Sagan are listed and defined below:

$N_* =$ the number of stars in our Milky Way galaxy. Based on surveys of representative regions of the sky, astronomers estimate this number to be "a few hundred billion." 4×10^{11} stars provides a middle-ground estimate.

$f_p =$ the fraction of stars that have planetary systems. Astronomers are detecting more and more planets each year. The planets discovered are primarily gas giant-types large enough to cause gravitational perturbations in the motion of their parent stars, but smaller planets probably occur there as well. Sagan estimated this fraction to be 0.33.

$n_e =$ the number of planets in a given system ecologically suited to life. In our own solar system both the Earth and Mars inhabit a "life zone" in which water can exist in all three phases at various times. In addition, there is reason to believe that the large moons of Jupiter, Ganymede and Callisto, might harbor subterranean oceans warm enough to harbor life. And there is always the chance for more exotic life forms within the atmosphere of gas giant planets. Sagan made $n_e = 2$.

$f_l =$ the fraction of life-suited planets on which life actually arises. While there is no solid evidence to provide a reliable number, we do know that the fossil remains of living cells appear within the first billion—perhaps the first half billion—years of Earth's history. This provides some encouragement that life may be a natural occurrence on suitable planets. But, we must also consider that life on Earth was limited to microscopic forms for the first 89% of its history.

Organismal complexity may require special circumstances and considerable time. Sagan makes an estimate of $f_l = 0.33$.

f_i = the fraction of life-infested planets on which intelligent life evolves. f_c = the fraction of planets with intelligent life where communicative, technical civilizations develop. Again, we have no basis of reference other than our own, Earth-based experience. Intelligent life here has only been around for a million years or so and science developed only in the last 500 years—both numbers are instants on the scale of geological time. Sagan estimates the product of f_i and f_c to be 0.01. Some scientists believe this number may not be nearly this large (3).

f_L = the fraction of a planet's lifetime that might be graced by a technologically minded civilization. This factor turns out to be the critical one in the equation. If technological civilizations tend to self-destruct in a few decades or centuries, then at any given time there might only be a handful of such civilizations active in an entire galaxy. If 1% of such civilizations could survive for tens of thousands of years or more, N might approach 10^7— approximately one technological civilization for every 200,000 suitable suns.

Michael Shermer, publisher of *Skeptic* magazine, in an article entitled "Why ET Hasn't Called" (Shermer, 2002), suggests that f_L is not that hard to calculate. Based on the longevity of Earth civilizations, he says that f_L should be equal to a number between 304.5 and 420.6 years. The larger figure is based on sixty civilizations going back to the Sumerians, the smaller is based on relatively modern civilizations (twenty-eight since the fall of Rome). Using these estimate N equals a number between 2.44 and 3.36.

A recent short story called "New Light on the Drake Equation," collected in *The Year's Best Science Fiction* (Dozois, 2002), describes a sixtyish Tom Kelly who devoted his entire career to listening for that elusive message from another civilization. During a drunken Thursday he has a ghostly visit by a former lover who helps re-energize his sense of wonder and purpose.

Finding Solutions to the Drake Equation

Divide your students into groups that each research one of the factors in the Drake Equation. Have each group present its findings and make recommendations for a number. The class can discuss each group's findings to see if further research is necessary. You will have to determine when the process is complete. Put some of your better students on the last factor in the equation and have them defend their determinations. If there is considerable controversy, calculate several values for N.

Stewart Brand published a book called *The Clock of the Long Now* (Brand, 1999). He contends that our society is much too short-sighted and needs to engage in a project that will focus people's attention on long-term survival. He proposes that we build an enormous mechanical clock in the desert southwest of the United States, perhaps as big as the Stonehenge monument, that would keep time for at least 10,000 years. Such a project would, he hopes, jolt people into considering deep time in the same way that seeing photographs of Earth from space helped jump-start the ecology movement. You may wish to look up his book or contact the Long Now Foundation, P.O. Box 29462, The Presidio, San Francisco, CA 94129 to get additional information.

Life science teachers need never fear that SF ignores their specialties in favor of the number-crunching hard sciences of physics and chemistry. In fact, life sciences are just now reaching a level of maturity that the physical sciences enjoyed in the nineteenth and early twentieth centuries and SF writers are jumping in with their usual audacity to speculate where current research will lead. Let such authors provide creative ledges to jump into the depths of new science fact.

NOTES

(1) Frank Herbert spent some twenty years elaborating on the *"Dune* universe" with the following sequels: *Dune Messiah* (1969), *Children of Dune* (1976) (which deals with the evolution of man into superman), *God Emperor of Dune* (1981), *Heretics of Dune* (1984), and *Chapter House Dune* (1985). Son Brian, with Kevin Anderson, has continued the story with *Dune, The Butlerian Jihad* (2002).

(2) Modern roboticist Helen Greiner, president and cofounder of iRobot Corporation, designs everything from high-tech toys to military robots. Her company's Packbots checked the soundness of remaining structures in the World Trade Center after their September 11 destruction. Her inspiration? The robot R2-D2 in *Star Wars*. She made up her mind to create a real R2-D2. Note, also, that her company name appears to be inspired by Asimov's *I, Robot* collection. Rodney A. Brooks, Chairman and Chief Technological Officer with iRobot Corp., says he was inspired by HAL in Arthur C. Clarke's *2001: A Space Odyssey*. He wrote *Flesh and Machines* (Pantheon Books, 2002), a fascinating look at the future of robotics.

(3) Peter Ward and Donald Brownlee in *Rare Earth: Why Complex Life Is Uncommon in the Universe* (Springer-Verlag New York, 2000) create an estimate more than four orders of magnitude smaller. They concede that microscopic life may be common, but they argue that complex metazoan life (including us) may be exceedingly rare because of the importance of plate tectonics, a moon that keeps Earth's axial tilt from wobbling too much, the importance of a metallic core, and other features that may not often coincide in planetary genesis.

REFERENCES

Aldiss, Brian. *Helliconia Spring*. New York: Atheneum, 1982.

Aldiss, Brian. *Helliconia Summer*. New York: Atheneum, 1983.

Aldiss, Brian. *Helliconia Winter*. New York: Atheneum, 1985.

Asimov, Isaac. *I, Robot*. New York: Signet Books, 1950.

Asimov, Isaac. *The Naked Sun*. New York: Bantam Books, 1957.

Asimov, Isaac. *The Rest of the Robots*. New York: Doubleday and Company, 1964.

Asimov, Isaac. *The Robots of Dawn*. New York: Doubleday and Company, 1983.

Asimov, Isaac. *Robots and Empire*. New York: Ballantine Books, 1985.

Blish, James. *The Seedling Stars and Galactic Cluster*. New York: New American Library, 1983.

Blish, James. "Surface Tension" in David G. Hartwell and Kathryn Cramer, eds. *The Ascent of Wonder: The Evolution of Hard Science Fiction*. New York: TOR, 1994, pp. 700–723.

Brand, Stewart. *The Clock of the Long Now*. New York: Basic Books, 1999.

Card, Orson Scott. *Ender's Game* (1984), *The Speaker for the Dead* (1986) in *Ender's War*. New York: Nelson Doubleday, 1986.

Clarke, Arthur C. *2001: A Space Odyssey*. New York: New American Library, 1968.

Clute, John, and Peter Nicholls. *The Encyclopedia of Science Fiction*. New York: St. Martin's Griffin, 1993 (update 1995).

Dick, Philip K. *Do Androids Dream of Electric Sheep?* New York: Signet Books, 1968.

Dozois, Gardner, ed. *The Year's Best Science Fiction*. New York: St. Martin's Griffin, 2002.

Grobstein, Clifford. *The Strategy of Life*. New York: W. H. Freeman, 1965.

Hartwell, David G., and Kathryn Cramer, eds. *The Ascent of Wonder: The Evolution of Hard SF.* New York: TOR, 1994.

Heinlein, Robert. *The Moon Is a Harsh Mistress*. New York: G.P. Putnam's Sons, 1968.

Herbert, Frank. *Dune*. New York: Ace Books, 1965.

Holdstock, Robert, and Malcolm Edwards. *Alien Landscapes*. New York: Mayflower Books, 1979.

Knight, Damon. *First Contact*. New York: Pinnacle Books, 1971.

Leinster, Murry. "First Contact" (1945) in *Contact*. New York: Paperback Library, 1963.

McDevitt, Jack. *Chindi*. New York: Ace Books, 2002.

McDevitt, Jack. *The Hercules Text*. New York: Berkley Publishing Group, 1986.

McDevitt, Jack. *Infinity Beach*. New York: Harper Prism, 2000.

Niven, Larry, and Jerry Pournelle. *The Mote in God's Eye*. New York: Simon & Schuster, 1974.

Sagan, Carl. *Contact*. New York: Simon & Schuster, 1985.

Sagan, Carl. *Cosmos*. New York: Random House, 1980 (pp. 299–302 discuss the Drake Equation).

Sagan, Carl. *Murmurs of Earth*. New York: Random House, 1978.

Shermer, Michael. "Why ET Hasn't Called" in *Scientific American* 287, no. 2, August 2002: 33.

Weir, Kirsten. "Robot Master" in *Current Science* 88, no. 13, February 28, 2003: 8–9.

Zindell, David. *Neverness*. New York: D. I. Fine, 1988.

ADDITIONAL READING

Ferris, Timothy. *Coming of Age in the Milky Way*. New York: William Morrow & Company, 1988.

Kauffman, Stewart. *At Home in the Universe*. New York: Oxford University Press, 1995.

Sagan, Carl. *Billions and Billions*. New York: Random House, 1997.

Ward, Peter Douglas, and Donald Brownlee. *Rare Earth: Why Complex Life Is Uncommon in the Universe*. New York: Springer-Verlag New York, 2000.

CHAPTER 9

SF Resources across Space-Time and the Curriculum

"Men have their times in little centuries for arts and fabulous monsters."
Loren Eiseley, "Men Have Their Times," in *Another Kind of Autumn*

Science fiction writers explore mystery and wonder in virtually all arenas of human endeavor and not just those subjects we might classify as the "hard sciences." This provides opportunities for you and other creative teachers to link science with diverse areas of the curriculum and even with recreational activities, like sports and games. Much good science fiction provides particularly rich mining territory for connections to history and math. Some SF writers, as we will see, acquired professional training or degrees in these fields while others studied history, in particular, for inspiration and insights into human nature.

One aspect of human nature involves anticipating—or second-guessing—the results of decisions contemplated or chosen some time in the past. What would have happened if I had married Linda instead of Sharon? If I had stayed in Michigan instead of Colorado? Scientists typically ask questions of nature in the form "If I do this, what will happen?" It seems natural that SF writers would explore such questions on the canvas of human—even geological—history and they have. Part of this chapter will discuss SF's ventures into alternate history, asking "what if " regarding the repercussions of alternate choices or outcomes of pivotal historical events. Another portion will look at how SF has used known history as a template for extrapolating the future. Do we learn from our mistakes or just repeat them on a grander scale? Finally, I will point to SF resources dealing with math, anthropology, and other areas explored by human curiosity, all of which may help you capture the attention of listless learners, who have not yet discovered that there are no boring subjects—just boring styles of presentation.

ALTERNATE HISTORY/PARALLEL WORLDS AND TIME TRAVEL

What If . . . ?

According to Harry Turtledove (1), a modern master in exploring alternative history through science fiction, the Roman historian Livy may have been the first to speculate in print about how history might have taken a different path. Livy (59 B.C.–A.D. 17), in his 142-book *History of Rome from Its Foundation* (of which only 35 books survive), wonders aloud what might have happened to the Roman Republic in the fourth century B.C. if Alexander the Great had focused his ambitions in their direction. As a patriotic Roman, he thought the Republic would have prevailed. Many subsequent historians have wondered how our modern world might look had certain key events unfolded differently.

Rewriting the American Civil War and the rise of Adolph Hitler in Germany have become clichés in the field. Clute and Nicholls in *The Encyclopedia of Science Fiction* attribute much of the early interest in these topics to two essays written in *Look* magazine in the early 1960s: "If the South Had Won the Civil War" (1960–61) by MacKinlay Kantor and "If Hitler Had Won World War II" (1961) by William L. Shirer. Writers have told tales about other pivotal events in history, including the Industrial Revolution, the Dark Ages, the Reformation, and the development of the atomic bomb. Harry Turtledove, mentioned above, even speculated on what things might have been like if *Homo erectus* and not American Indians had been in North America to meet exploring Europeans ("A Different Flesh," 1988).

Turtledove attributes his own obsession with alternate history to a book he read as an impressionable teen by L. Sprague de Camp called *Lest Darkness Fall* (1949) in which an involuntary time traveler finds himself in sixth-century Rome and subsequently tries to prevent the occurrence of the Dark Ages. He even credits de Camp as the impetus for his acquisition of a Ph.D. in Byzantine history—certainly a testimonial for SF stimulating academic interest. Turtledove recently edited (with Martin H. Greenberg) an excellent book called *The Best Alternate History Stories of the 20th Century* (2001). In it he includes stories by Kim Stanley Robinson, Larry Niven, Greg Bear, Gregory Benford, Poul Anderson, and others. One of Michael Crichton's recent thrillers, *Timeline* (1999), deals with the adventures of scientists who travel back to fourteenth-century feudal France.

Perhaps science fiction has come full circle and helped create a climate that allows historians to speculate more freely about alternate histories. I came across a book called *What If? 2* (2001), edited by Robert Crowley, in which historians speculate on such things as what would have happened if Socrates had died at the Battle of Delium in 424 B.C. and not inspired Plato to turn to philosophy, or what if Pontius Pilate had spared Jesus? Would Christianity have been the same without a crucifixion? Or what if Pizarro had not found potatoes in Peru? Could the failure to discover a prolific and nutritious vegetable have rewritten the history of the Western world?

Parallel Worlds and the Nature of Time

Sometimes SF plunges us into an alternate vision of history with no explanation. Other times we arrive via some sort of time travel mechanism, the nature of which depends on how the author chooses to portray time itself. Is what we experience at this moment a discrete point on a temporal string, so that we could visit other points (past or future) on the string if we knew how? Is time like a burning fuse with the present the point of combustion and the past an unreachable trail of ashes? Could time be like the layers of an onion with an infinite series of parallel timelines created by every possible sequence of events? Or could time be some sort of finished sculpture, with the present moment experienced like the touch of a finger along its surface? It's hard not to mix metaphors trying to bend our minds around this slippery concept.

If time is like a string—or a chain of dominoes—then visiting the past could change everything that happens subsequently. Ray Bradbury produced a classic story in that vein with "A Sound of Thunder" (1952). A time-traveling tourist steps off the designated path, crushing a butterfly that lived in the distant past. This minor event caused a ripple in time that resulted in drastic changes when the protagonist returned to his present.

If time can be so easily mucked up, it might need protection and regulation. Poul Anderson wrote a series of "Time Patrol" stories based on the assumption that a future human society was keeping historical events on the right path. Most of these stories were collected in *The Time Patrol* (1991) and *The Shield of Time* (1990). "Death and the Knight," a story about a temporal agent who nearly subverts history by falling in love with a fourteenth-century local, appears in Poul Anderson's recent autobiographical collection, *Going for Infinity* (2002). You may also wish to look up Isaac Asimov's *The End of Eternity* (1955) and John Brunner's *Times without Number* (1969).

The notion of parallel worlds similar to, but distinct from, our own extends far back in myth and folklore. The concept was given some scientific credibility with speculations about "multi-verses" resulting from some of the enigmas of quantum mechanics where events, at the elementary particle level at least, can somehow depend on whether or not they are observed. For a look at parallel, but linked worlds where physical laws are not quite the same, check out Isaac Asimov's *The Gods Themselves* (1972). Larry Niven in "All the Myriad Ways" (1971) (collected in *The Best Alternate History Stories of the Twentieth Century*) shows how all those parallel worlds could drive you crazy.

Even geniuses have had trouble with the nature of time. Newton proclaimed time to be fixed and immutable while the speed of a beam of light should vary depending on how observers moved relative to it. Einstein revealed that it is the speed of light that is constant and it is time that may move fast or slow depending on the relative motions of the timekeepers. In practice, the difference is hard to detect except at speeds that are a considerable fraction of the speed of light, but the variability of time has been confirmed by many experiments in communications technology and particle physics and measured with atomic clocks placed aboard satellites (2). Today, these relativistic, nanosecond effects are instrumental in keeping Global Positioning System (GPS) satellites on track (3).

The speed of light is not only a constant, but an apparent speed limit, because if a physical object actually traveled at the speed of light, its mass would become infinite. I say apparent speed limit because in the early sixties several researchers suggested that a particle that *must travel* faster than the speed of light wouldn't violate any of the precepts of relativistic physics (Clute and Nicholls, 1995, pp. 1199–1200). Such a particle, called a tachyon, would have an imaginary mass—in the same sense that the square root of minus one is an imaginary number. Tachyons would have some disconcerting properties, such as appearing to move backward through time. Or, a negative-energy tachyon moving backward in time might be interpreted as a positive-energy tachyon moving forward in time. Could tachyons somehow be used to communicate between different time periods? Physicist/writer Gregory Benford ran with this idea in his novel *Timescape* (1980), in which scientists detect a tachyonic message from the future urging them to act in ways that will forestall a coming disaster.

When History Is the Focus

Sometimes the mechanism of time travel is fairly irrelevant to the writer's mission. It simply becomes the vehicle that places characters into the past or future as the most effective way to highlight some human truth. History teachers could easily use this form of science fiction to resurrect the past for students. Connie Willis is very adept at creating these kinds of stories. In her first solo novel, *Lincoln's Dreams* (1987), which won the John W. Campbell Memorial Award, she transports her characters back to the American Civil War through psychic connections between them and General Robert E. Lee and his horse, Traveller. The story is not an endorsement of psychic phenomena, but a tale of love and war that makes the Civil War seem close and immediate.

In the 1980s Willis wrote a number of short stories with time travel themes involving a future historiography research unit based at Cambridge University that sends its people back to study artifacts in place and sometimes make some temporal changes—like saving St. Paul's Cathedral during Germany's bombing of London during World War II. Again, the university's time machine is peripheral to the human tales told. A number of these stories were collected in *Fire Watch* (1982). *Doomsday Book* (1992), an excellent novel using the same time travel premise, sends a young female student, Kivrin, to the fourteenth century. Inadvertently, she arrives in the middle of the plague years of the Black Death. The institute mounts a rescue mission while Kivrin attempts to survive as a woman traveling alone. In the process, she keeps hope alive for people who have none in what seems to be an era of dark judgment.

Dr. Joanna Lander in Willis' book *Passage* (2001) seeks to learn more about the "Near Death Experience" by studying people who have been declared clinically dead and then recovered. She gets involved with research studies using a psychoactive drug that mimics the effects and seems to place her on the decks of the sinking *Titanic*. This book addresses complex issues of life, death, and the afterlife while recreating a dramatic, historical event.

Student Activities

- Have students write their own "what if?" stories about an historical event—either typical alternate-history tales or stories set in a universe that obeys different physical laws.

- Have students create a real timeline for a given period in time that they are studying and then a fictional timeline based on a change in one key event. If Newton had never lived, would other scientists eventually have discovered his laws? How long might it have taken? How would other events in history have been affected?

- Guide students in creating a technology timeline that spans their own and perhaps their parents' lifetimes. Have them speculate on how their lives would be different if some key technology had never been developed.

HISTORY AS A TEMPLATE FOR THE FUTURE

Science fiction writers often look to history to provide them with inspiration and patterns of human behavior. The last 10,000 years of sporadically recorded history provide numerous examples of human achievement and folly. The invention of agriculture provided sufficient food to allow human populations to increase. The templates of behavior developed over millennia of wandering small tribes of hunter/gatherers had to be tossed aside in favor of other forms of social management. Strong leaders built kingdoms, then empires, which sometimes created impressive monuments, but were often in conflict with other, similar societies. Eventually, broader education led to experience with more egalitarian group management, but with episodes of conflict still exceeding examples of cooperation. There is no reason to think that behavior established over centuries and untold millennia will change as quickly as the change from using clubs to using remote controls. Besides, we tell stories—even future stories—to learn something about ourselves, so writing about creatures with totally alien motivations, unless they shed light on the human condition, provides no useful insights.

The Rise and Fall of Empires

Isaac Asimov read widely in history, devouring each of Will and Ariel Durant's *The Story of Civilization* volumes as they were published. In fact, in his autobiography, *In Memory Yet Green* (1979), Asimov says in a footnote, "After I had read the first one and heard he was planning a multivolume history—five volumes was the original plan—I felt worried. I knew he was in his forties and I carefully noted in my diary that I hoped he would live long enough to complete the set. He did." Asimov also read Gibbon's *Rise and Fall of the Roman Empire* and proposed to John W. Campbell in the early 1940s a story about a galactic empire loosely based on the Roman model. The idea evolved into a series that extended over a twenty-year period, which was assembled as the *Foundation Trilogy* in 1963. In 1965 it was given a Hugo Award as "The Best All-Time Series."

Cyclic History

Author James Blish studied Oswald Spengler (1880–1936) (Clute and Nicholls, 1995, p. 135), an historian who emphasized the cyclic nature of history. Blish also grew up during the Depression and the time of the migration of farmers during the dust bowl years. He conceived a human future where entire cities roamed the stars using antigravity devices called "spindizzies." Four novels were eventually collected as *Cities in Flight* (1970): *They Shall Have Stars, A Life for the Stars, Earthman Come Home,* and *The Triumph of Time.* In the last volume our present universe ends, but the mayor of the last wandering city ultimately serves as the nucleus for the rebirth of the next universe.

Walter M. Miller Jr.'s career, spanning more than a half century, uses science fiction to highlight the cyclic nature of human folly within the context of formal religion and Man's relationship to God—a fairly rare approach in science fiction. His most famous novel, *A Canticle for Leibowitz* (1959), begins 600 years after a nuclear holocaust nearly destroys the human race. St. Leibowitz was a twentieth-century physicist who founded a Catholic order of monks and charged them with saving a body of knowledge through a dark age of barbarism and antiscience sentiment. Through the eyes of three monks who live about 500 years apart, we see society rebuild itself only to fall victim to yet another war. A starship leaves to colonize a nearby star before this second fall of civilization. Miller's view of human nature is rather dark, but the writing is vivid, ironic, and honest.

The Evolution of Civilization

Perhaps cultures, like organisms, evolve. As time goes by, we learn something from our mistakes and move from cultural infancy to maturity. With scientific advancement as part of the mix, we as a species learn to control natural processes and manipulate far greater amounts of energy—a process with inherent dangers as well as rewards. In 1964, Soviet astronomer N. S. Kardashev proposed that we might be able to define civilizations by the amount of energy they use (4). Our civilization, for example, might be defined as a Type I civilization, capable of harnessing the fossil fuel reserves of an entire planet. A Type II civilization might be able to tap virtually all the energy of its home star. Theoretical physicist Freeman Dyson suggested that such a civilization might be hard to detect if it built a ring or sphere of structures completely around its star and blocked off its light. The concept of such a Dyson Sphere (proposed in *Science,* 1960) has been used by a number of science fiction writers, including Larry Niven in his Ringworld series. A Type III civilization could utilize the energy of an entire galaxy and its activities might be detectable anywhere in the universe.

So what might an advanced civilization do if it came in contact with a more primitive one? On Earth, contact between two cultures with greatly differing levels of technology has been invariably disastrous for the more primitive culture. If the latter culture is not destroyed outright, its spiritual underpinnings and confidence often decay and its youth tend to be absorbed into the more advanced civilization. Must this be the case? Might a truly advanced civilization appreciate the unique qualities of a developing culture and develop a "helping hand" or at least a "hands off " policy?

Author Sylvia Louise Engdahl has explored the concept of a benevolent, older civilization working behind the scenes to preserve "youngling cultures" in several of her novels. Perhaps her best known title is *Enchantress from the Stars* (1970), a Newberry Honor Book discussed briefly in Chapter 1. A young girl, Elana, the daughter of a Federation anthropologist, has stowed aboard her father's vessel on assignment to Andrecia, a planet with a prescientific native culture in danger of extinction at the hands of a Youngling spacefaring civilization. Elana becomes a key player in saving the indigenous culture without revealing her true nature to either them or the aggressor civilization, but she must learn some hard lessons about love and sacrifice in the process. This book, along with its sequel, *The Far Side of Evil* (1972), should appeal to both boys and girls in your classrooms. In the latter book, Elana, on her first official assignment as a Federation agent, must observe a culture living through their Critical Stage of potential extinction through nuclear war without revealing herself—a situation that puts her in mortal danger.

Activities

- Take a historical event you are studying and have students rewrite it as it might unfold in our present or future. Focus not just on a sequence of events, but on the human motivations that caused the events to unfold as they did. You may want to have them read excerpts from *The Foundation Trilogy* or *Cities in Flight* stories and point out their connections to Roman history and the Depression era years in the United States.

- Have students read one of Engdahl's books. Have them compare and contrast the Federation's policy of "anonymous intervention" with the Spanish contact with the Aztecs in Mexico or Captain Cook's encounter with New Zealanders.

- Have students analyze what their family throws into the trash during one week from the point of view of some alien anthropologists. Define the physical and cultural characteristics of the aliens first, then attempt to look at our trash through their sense organs and biases.

SF AND MATHEMATICS

Other Dimensions

Flatland by Edwin A. Abbott has become a classic since it was first published in 1884. It describes the adventures of two-dimensional creatures as they encounter "invasions" by three-dimensional visitors. It serves as a great way to introduce students to aspects of relativity and multiple spacial dimensions. It also offers unique ways to visualize multidimensional forms like tesseracts and hyperspheres. Dover Books (1952) published an inexpensive paperback.

Ian Stewart, Professor of Mathematics at the University of Warwick, has published a modern sequel called *Flatterland* (Perseus Publishing, 2001) (5). Victoria Line is the great-great-granddaughter of A. Square in Abbott's book. She helps lead the reader to a greater understanding of the shape and origins of the universe, the nature of space, time, and matter, as well as modern geometries and their applications.

Rudy Rucker also wrote a short story called "Message Found in a Copy of *Flatland*," which is reprinted in *The Ascent of Wonder: The Evolution of Hard SF* by David Hartwell and Kathryn Cramer (1994). Rucker tells the story of Robert Ackley, who writes of his entrapment in Flatland after an encounter with a woman in a Pakistani restaurant. The same collection features an excellent story by Greg Bear called "Tangents" (1986). It portrays in a convincing fashion what it might be like if we caught the attention of higher-dimensional beings (in this case through the venue of music).

In 1940, Robert Heinlein wrote a story "And He Built a Crooked House" that details the problems of an architect who builds a house shaped like a tesseract that accidentally folds up into the fourth dimension during an earthquake. Charles Hinton, a British mathematician and contemporary of Albert Einstein, coined the term "tesseract" to describe what an unfolded hypercube would look like in our three-dimensional universe. Just as an "unfolded" cube in a 2-D universe would look like a cross made of six squares, an unfolded hypercube in our universe would look like a cross made of eight cubes. (See Fig. 9.1.)

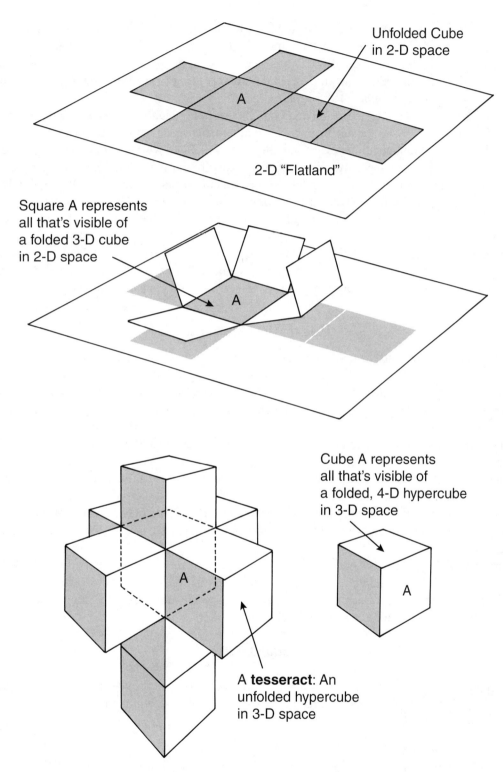

Figure 9.1. Two-dimensional beings in "Flatland" can only visualize a cube in its "unfolded" shape: that of a cross made of six squares. Likewise, human beings inhabiting a three-dimensional universe can only visualize a hypercube in its unfolded state: a tesseract made of eight cubes. When they are folded into the fourth dimension, all we can see is a cube.

Mathematics and Communication

Math as a universal language is another theme used in science fiction. Kim Stanley Robinson uses the concept of harmonies in mathematics in *The Memory of Whiteness* (1985) Arthur C. Clarke employs the mathematics of fractals as a key element in *The Ghost from the Grand Banks* (1990). Carl Sagan embedded information in the nonrepeating digits to the right of the decimal point in pi in his novel *Contact* (1985).

Ursula K. LeGuin created the mathematician Shevek in her Hugo- and Nebula-winning novel *The Dispossessed* (1974) Shevek invents the mathematics necessary to create the ansible, a faster-than-light communication device that allows the inhabited worlds in our corner of the universe to converse instantaneously. With LeGuin's background in anthropology, her stories are rich in human detail and historical parallels with Earth cultures (see Chapter 4, "Women in SF"). *The Dispossessed* is the fifth novel set in a common universe (but at the earliest point in time in the series) where an ancient planet called Hain seeded habitable worlds in the galaxy with humans.

Mathematics is more central to the theme in David Zindell's *Neverness* (1988). A mathematician himself, Zindell successfully conveys the joy and excitement of mathematical discovery through a protagonist who can only map "space windows" with elegant theorems.

Recreating Flatland

Edwin Abbott provides all the details you need to have your students recreate a version of "Flatland." It will provide them with practical experience using rulers, compasses, and protractors and they can "play" while learning some important math skills and concepts. *Flatland* (the book) is also an amusing social satire of nineteenth-century attitudes that helps put our own biases in perspective.

Flatlanders are lines or regular polygons with a length or breadth of not more than twelve inches. I suggest you work at one-quarter scale so that a businessman, for example, would be an equilateral triangle with 3" sides. A woman is a 3" line. Professional men are squares and pentagons. A soldier is an isosceles triangle with two sides of 3" and one side of 1/8". Nobility are regular polygons of six sides or more and priests are circles. Each generation of four sides or more produces children with one additional side. Working-class triangles almost always breed more triangles!

Create a model of Flatland out of a large piece of cardboard or foamcore, perhaps 36"×48". Have students make the individual classes of characters out of heavy paper or cardboard using rulers, compasses, and protractors. Women can be pipe cleaners cut in 3" lengths with their forward-facing "eye" colored with a highlighter or marker.

Flatland Rules

- There are the normal four compass directions, with north being the direction from which rain comes. A weak attractive force pulls from the south. No sun is visible. Light is mysterious and pervasive.

- Houses are regular pentagons with a large men's door on the west side and a small women's door on the east. (The roof faces north.) Houses of sharper angles are prohibited.

- Women, by custom, pass on the north side of men on a path. (Women are dangerous because they are points when met head-on and can impale the unwary! Their rear ends are dim and hard to see.)

Activities

Making Flatland and Her People

Have the class create a version of Flatland with a village of several houses, a forest, a school, a church, and a fort, with room for paths to each area. (Trees can be semicircles with vertical rectangles beneath, something like mushrooms.) Point out, as Abbott does, that every person (except a woman, head-on) appears to be a straight line. This will be easy to visualize when students look along Flatland edge-on. Abbott describes several ways for people to recognize one another.

1. By hearing: Women, for example, must maintain a "peace cry" when in public places.

2. By feeling: Flatlanders become very good at recognizing, by touch, the angles of someone they encounter, and thus determining the status of the individual.

3. By sight: In a slight fog one can see edges on either side of a vertex fading away in the distance. A circular priest seems clear and sharp only in the middle and fades gradually to either side. In the past Flatlanders painted themselves for color recognition, but the practice fell out of favor as confusion may result when one class assumes the colors of another.

Once Flatland has been created, you could devise a mathematical board game. Students could start along a path from opposite ends of Flatland. When they encounter another player, they must announce the number of degrees in the forward angle of the polygon they encounter before proceeding—and so on. You can become inventive to reinforce certain ideas or skills.

Designing Buildings

Have students design various public and private buildings to accommodate the various classes. They could design a school, church, fort, or four-bedroom house (See Fig. 9.2 for the design of A Square's house in Flatland.)

Invasion from Spaceland

Using various three-dimensional objects, have students describe the appearance in Flatland as the object passes into and through their world. Afterward, they can better visualize the four-dimensional intrusion into 3-D space described in "Tangents" by Greg Bear.

Much of the science fiction described in this chapter—and throughout this book—formalizes a process that human beings already employ with great success: imagining alternatives to contemplated and past actions and visualizing the universe with a different set of starting assumptions. Science fiction writers often immerse themselves in history, art, sports—the whole range of human activities—both for recreation and to make their fictional worlds come alive on the page. You can find imaginative literature that addresses the interests of nearly every child and use that as a lever to turn apathy into excitement and to turn indifference into that sense of boundless wonder that science fiction creates so well. And, as teachers, I'll wager that you can already anticipate all the new things you will learn yourself along the way and eagerly await the opportunity to share your excitement with students.

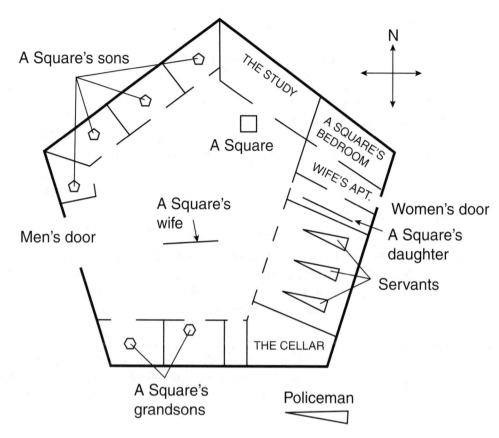

Figure 9.2. A Square's House in Flatland.

NOTES

(1) Harry Turtledove makes his observations in the introduction to *The Best Alternative History Stories of the 20th Century* (Ballantine Publishing Group, 2001).

(2) In 1977, scientists demonstrated time variance when an atomic clock aboard an American satellite ran slower (on the order of a few billionths of a second) than reference clocks at the Naval Research Laboratory in Washington, DC (Langone, 2000, p. 21).

(3) The effects of general relativity and not just special relativity are important in GPS technology (Panek, 2002, p. 51).

(4) Asimov discusses this topic in *Extraterrestrial Civilizations* (p. 249).

(5) Abbott himself also wrote a sequel called *Sphereland.*

REFERENCES

Abbott, Edwin A. *Flatland* (1884). New York: Dover Publications, 1952.

Anderson, Poul. "Death and the Knight" in *Going for Infinity: A Literary Journey.* New York: TOR/Tom Doherty Associates Book, 2002.

Anderson, Poul. *The Shield of Time.* New York: Tom Doherty Associates, 1990.

Anderson, Poul. *The Time Patrol.* New York: Tom Doherty Associates, 1991.

Asimov, Isaac. *The End of Eternity.* New York: Doubleday & Company, 1955.

Asimov, Isaac. *Extraterrestrial Civilizations.* New York: Crown Publishers, 1979.

Asimov, Isaac. *Foundation Trilogy.* New York: Doubleday & Company, 1963.

Asimov, Isaac. *The Gods Themselves.* New York: Doubleday & Company, 1972.

Asimov, Isaac. *In Memory Yet Green.* New York: Doubleday & Company, 1979.

Bear, Greg. "Tangents" (1986) in David G Hartwell and Kathryn Cramer, eds. *The Ascent of Wonder: The Evolution of Hard SF*. New York: TOR, 1994.

Benford, Gregory. *Timescape*. New York: Pocket Books, 1980.

Blish, James. *Cities in Flight* (1970). Woodstock: Overlook Press, 2000.

Bradbury, Ray. "A Sound of Thunder" (1952). Sound recording. Niagara Falls, NY: Darkin Hayes Publishers, 1994.

Brunner, John. *Times without Number*. New York: Ace Publishing Corp., 1969.

Clarke, Arthur C. *The Ghost from the Grand Banks*. New York: Bantam Books, 1990.

Clute, John, and Peter Nicholls. *The Encyclopedia of Science Fiction*. New York: St. Martin's Griffin, 1993 (update 1995).

Crowley, Robert. *What If? 2*. New York: G. P. Putnam's Sons, 2001.

de Camp, L. Sprague. *Lest Darkness Fall* (1949). New York: Pyramid Books, 1963.

Engdahl, Sylvia Louise. *Enchantress from the Stars* (1970). New York: Walker & Co., 2001.

Engdahl, Sylvia Louise. *The Far Side of Evil*. New York: Atheneum, 1972.

Heinlein, Robert A. "And He Built a Crooked House" (1940) in *6 X H*. New York: Pyramid Books, 1971, p. 172.

Kaku, Michio. *Hyperspace*. New York: Oxford University Press, 1994.

Langone, John. *The Mystery of Time*. Washington, DC: National Geographic Books, 2000.

LeGuin, Ursula. *The Dispossessed*. New York: Harper & Row, 1974.

Miller, Walter M. *A Canticle for Leibowitz* (1959). New York: Bantam Books, 1960.

Niven, Larry. *All the Myriad Ways*. New York: Ballantine Books, 1971.

Niven, Larry. *Ringworld*. New York: Ballantine Books, 1970.

Panek, Richard. "And Then There Was Light" in *Natural History* 111, no. 9, November 2002: 46.

Robinson, Kim Stanley. *The Memory of Whiteness: A Scientific Romance*. New York: Tom Doherty Associates, 1985.

Rucker, Rudy. "Message Found in a Copy of *Flatland*" (1983) in David G. Hartwell and Kathryn Cramer, eds. *The Ascent of Wonder: The Evolution of Hard SF*. New York: TOR, 1994, p. 434.

Sagan, Carl. *Contact*. New York: Simon & Schuster, 1985.

Stewart, Ian. *Flatterland*. Cambridge, MA: Perseus Publishing, 2001.

Turtledove, Harry. *A Different Flesh*. New York: Congdon & Weed. Distributed by Contempory Books in assoc. with Davis Publications, 1988.

Turtledove, Harry, and Martin Greenberg, eds. *The Best Alternative History Stories of the 20th Century*. New York: Ballantine Publishing Group, 2001.

Willis, Connie. *Doomsday Book*. New York: Bantam Books, 1992.

Willis, Connie. *Fire Watch* (1982). New York: Bluejay Books, 1985.

Willis, Connie. *Lincoln's Dreams* (1987). New York: Bantam Books, 1992.

Willis, Connie. *Passage*. New York: Bantam Books, 2001.

Zindell, David. *Neverness*. New York: D. I. Fine, 1988.

ADDITIONAL READING

Cuppy, Will. *The Decline and Fall of Practically Everybody*. New York: Dell Publishing Co., 1950.

Durant, Will, and Ariel Durant. *The Lessons of History*. New York: Simon & Schuster, 1968.

Fernandez-Armesto, Felipe. *Millennium, A History of the Last Thousand Years*. New York: Scribner, 1995.

Rucker, Rudolf v. B. *Geometry, Relativity, and the Fourth Dimension*. New York: Dover Publications, 1977.

Wedgewood, C. V. *The Spoils of Time, a World History from the Dawn of Civilization through the Early Renaissance*. New York: Doubleday & Co., 1985.

APPENDIX I

Resources for Keeping the Facts and the Fiction Straight

Before warping your way across the galaxy or rebuilding dinosaurs from ancient DNA, you may want to consult the experts on certain points of scientific study. This appendix looks at several user-friendly resources.

GUIDEBOOKS FROM MEDIA-SAVVY SCIENTISTS

The Physics of *Star Trek* (Basic Books, 1995)

Author: Lawrence M. Krauss, physicist and Ambrose Swasey professor of physics, professor of astronomy, and chairman of the Department of Physics at Case Western Reserve University.

Book sections include: "A Cosmic Poker Game," which discusses the physics of inertial dampers and tractor beams, paving the way for time travel, warp speed, deflector shields, wormholes, and other spacetime oddities.

"Matter Matter Everywhere" explores transporter beams, warp drives, dilithium crystals, matter-antimatter engines, and the holodeck.

"The Invisible Universe, or Things That Go Bump in the Night" speaks of things that may exist but are not yet seen—extraterrestrial life, multiple dimensions, and an exotic zoo of other physics possibilities and impossibilities.

Beyond *Star Trek* (Perennial, 1998)

Author: Lawrence M. Krauss.

Topics discussed include the fuel requirements for travel to other star systems, the probability of life and how it relates to the Drake equation (see Chapter 8), various end-of-the-world scenarios, and human-versus-machine intelligence, among other topics. Krauss includes an interesting discussion that attempts to resolve some of the apparent quantum mechanical paradoxes that result from trying to use metaphors fabricated by our "common sense" brains operating at dimensions ruled by Newtonian physics.

The Science of *Jurassic Park* and *The Lost World* (Basic Books, 1997)

Authors: Rob Desalle, associate curator at the American Museum of Natural History in New York, and David Lindley, a physicist and editor at *Science News*.

The authors point out various "liberties" taken by the movies' creators: amber mines are usually in scrub-covered hill country, not in caves near a river; Dominican amber is the wrong age for dinosaur-biting mosquitos; biting insects in amber are extremely rare; most of the "star" dinosaurs were of Cretaceous not Jurassic age, and so forth, but their main focus is to take the reader through a "Manhattan Project" for building a living dinosaur to show the immense difficulty of such an endeavor.

Star Trek **on the Brain: Alien Minds, Human Minds** (W. H. Freeman, 1998)

Authors: Robert Sekuler, professor of psychology at Brandeis University, and Randolph Blake, professor of psychology at Vanderbilt University.

The authors use a study of *Star Trek* aliens to provide insights into the brains and minds of *Homo sapiens*. Extensive notes at the end of the book refer the reader to relevant scientific studies. For non-*Star Trek* fans, there are mini-bios of the characters mentioned. The authors list each episode they reference and identify it as Original Series, the Next Generation, Deep Space 9, Voyager, or one of the *Star Trek* movies. They also point the reader toward various *Star Trek* information sources: *The Star Trek Encyclopedia* by Michael and Denise Okuda, *The Nitpicker's Guide* series by Phil Farrand, *Star Trek: The Next Generation Companion,* and *Trek: The Unauthorized A–Z* by Hal Schuster and Wendy Rathbone.

RAIDING WRITERS' RESOURCES

Writer's Digest Books, a book-publishing affiliate of *Writer's Digest Magazine,* has produced an entire series of books for the aspiring and practicing SF writer edited by Ben Bova. Bova is the author of ninety books of his own, some fact and some science fiction, and he was a former editor at both *Omni* and *Analog Science Fiction* magazines. For each book in the series Bova teamed up with a scientist/SF author.

Aliens and Alien Societies (Writer's Digest Books, 1995)

Author: Stanley Schmidt, editor of *Analog Science Fiction and Fact* and Ph.D. in physics at Heidelberg College.

This guide for fashioning believable aliens and their societies will especially appeal to biology teachers because creating believable aliens involves sketching out the geological history, biochemistry, and evolution of their planet in addition to the specifics of their history, social structures, and languages—necessarily patterned on what we know about life on Earth.

World-Building (Writer's Digest Books, 1996)

Author: Stephen L. Gillett holds a Ph.D. in geology from SUNY Stony Brook and is a research associate at Mackay School of Mines, University of Nevada at Reno. He has written science fiction short stories as well as science articles for *Analog* and *Amazing* magazines.

Chapter titles: "The Astronomical Setting," "Making a Planet," "The Earth," "The Ancient Earth," "The Other Planets," "Stars and Suns," and "Not as We Know It." He covers some of the particulars for calculating horizon distances, orbits, seasonal changes, and so forth that will fit in nicely with physics and mathematical topics you may wish to cover. He goes into details of planet formation, discusses what we know about our own planet (both modern and ancient), and examines space-probe-garnered details about the outer planets of our system. The last chapter looks at some of the more exotic planetary settings.

Time Travel (Writer's Digest Books, 1997)

Author: Paul J. Nahin, professor of electrical engineering at the University of New Hampshire.

Topics discussed: special relativity, time travel into the past, hyperspace, time as a fourth dimension, the block universe, causal time loops, and other topics. Time travel mechanisms include rotating cylinders, wormholes, exotic matter, and cosmic strings. Nahin also explores multiple time tracks and parallel worlds.

The last chapter specifically addresses reading the physics literature for story ideas. The book also contains a glossary of selected terms and concepts, bibliography, and index.

Other titles: *Time Machines, Time Travel in Physics, Metaphysics, and Science Fiction.*

Space Travel: A Writer's Guide to the Science of Interplanetary and Interstellar Travel
(Writer's Digest Books, 1997)

Authors: Ben Bova and Anthony R. Lewis, best known as a writer of bibliographical and reference works.

   This book includes much good information on rockets, the environment of space, living and working in space, possible space industries, and potential space habitats that might be built and maintained at two of the gravitationally stable LaGrange points in lunar orbit. The authors also examine what life on our moon might be like. The chapter on starships discusses concepts like generations ships (where several generations would live and die on board before arrival at a distant sun), lightsails and magsails (ships powered by solar radiation), sleeping to the stars (suspended animation), and various faster-than-light possibilities. *Space Travel* also contains a bibliography, list of references, glossary, and index.

POPULAR SCIENCE BOOKS

A number of fine science popularizers can make more teacher-accessible a discipline you are not on journal-reading terms with. Once you've discovered a writer who speaks to you and your interests, search Amazon.com or other online bookstores to see what they've published lately.

Physics and Astronomy

Stephen Hawking

Stephen Hawking holds down Isaac Newton's old chair at Cambridge (The Lucasian Professor of Mathematics) and has been a leader in extending the work of Albert Einstein and other physicists. His titles have been best sellers and include *A Brief History of Time, From the Big Bang to Black Holes* (Bantam, 1988), *The Illustrated Brief History of Time* (1996), *Black Holes and Baby Universes and Other Essays* (Bantam, 1993), and *The Universe in a Nutshell* (Bantam, 2001). John Boslough also wrote a biography of Hawking and his work called *Stephen Hawking's Universe* (William Morrow & Co., 1985).

Richard P. Feynman

Richard Feynman worked on the atomic bomb project during World War II, won the Nobel prize for his work with subatomic particles, and remained a lifelong learner and teacher. He was a bit of a troublemaker and pot-stirrer—kind of the Loki of atomic physicists. His humor, gift for metaphor, and productivity yielded a number of books and lecture series that have been actively marketed since his death. Books include *QED: The Strange Theory of Light and Matter* (Princeton University Press, 1985) and *The Meaning of It All* (Perseus Books, 1998). Also look up James Gleick's *Genius* (Pantheon, 1992) for an entertaining biography.

Timothy Ferris

Timothy Ferris writes with elegance and style, dripping quotables from every page. A teacher of both science writing and astronomy, he has won many writing awards and honors. His titles include *Coming of Age in the Milky Way* (William Morrow & Co., 1988) and *The Mind's Sky, Human*

Intelligence in a Cosmic Context (Bantam, 1992). *Seeing in the Dark* (Simon & Schuster, 2002) shows the important contribution of amateur astronomers to the space sciences and demonstrates how the adventure of science can sustain you for a lifetime.

Carl Sagan

Carl Sagan was the Director of the Laboratory for Planetary Studies and David Duncan Professor of Astronomy and Space Sciences at Cornell when he hosted the popular PBS series *Cosmos*. The book by the same name was published by Random House in 1980. In 1977, two *Voyager* spacecraft left Earth with a plaque and "messages from Earth" he helped design. The book commemorating that project was *Murmurs of Earth* (Random House, 1978).

Other titles by Sagan include *Contact* (1985), *Intelligent Life in the Universe* (1966), and *The Cosmic Connection: An Extraterrestrial Perspective* (1973). Not long before his death he wrote *Billions and Billions, Thoughts on Life and Death at the Brink of the Millennium* (Random House, 1997) and *The Demon-Haunted World* (Ballantine Books, 1998) in which he offers tools to debunk pseudoscience and unreason in making decisions in the modern world.

Isaac Asimov

Science fiction writer, chemistry professor, and prolific writer of over a hundred books, Isaac Asimov wrote a three-volume guide to physics that is showing some age, but may still be useful: *Understanding Physics I, II, and III* (George Allen & Unwin Ltd., London, 1966).

Also note some of the nonfiction titles relating to the physical sciences I recommend at the end of Chapter 6.

Life Science/Natural History

Many fine writers have made a contribution to understanding the life sciences. I have lumped a lot of subjects under this broad category, but it should give you a sampling of representative resources.

Edward O. Wilson

Edward Wilson is another practicing scientist (at Harvard) who writes with both knowledge and elegance. He won the Pulitzer Prize for *On Human Nature* (1978) and shared the Pulitzer with Bert Holldobler for *The Ants* (Belknap Press, 1990). A shorter narrative aimed at the general public is *Journey of the Ants* (Belknap, 1994). Wilson is probably best known for *Sociobiology, the New Synthesis* (1975) where he proposes many genetic underpinnings for social behavior in humans and other animals. Wilson has also been an outspoken proponent of maintaining biodiversity to sustain Earth's rich web of life. *The Diversity of Life* (Belknap Press, 1992) eloquently outlines his plea. He was awarded the Audubon Medal in 1995 for his contributions to conservation and environmental protection.

Stephen Jay Gould

Stephen Jay Gould wrote a column on evolution for *Natural History Magazine* for many years. He wrote with insight and humor, but could get a little academically "dense" on occasion. His essays were compiled into a series of books. He also authored/edited a fine book on paleontology called *The Book of Life, an Illustrated History of the Evolution of Life on Earth* (W. W. Norton & Co., 1993). He was co-originator (with Niles Eldridge) of the "punctuated equilibrium" theory that proposed that evolutionary change proceeded in fits and starts largely choreographed by extinction events in Earth's history.

Lynn Margulis

Lynn Margulis, Distinguished Professor at the University of Massachusetts, Amherst, produced, with Karlene V. Schwartz, a valuable book that highlighted the changes in thinking about how the living world is related. *Five Kingdoms, an Illustrated Guide to the Phyla of Life on Earth* (W. H. Freeman & Co.) first appeared in 1982 and was updated in 1998. Margulis' once-controversial theory that mitochondria and chloroplasts in higher organisms resulted from the symbiosis of prokaryotic microbes with early eukaryotic cells is now part of mainstream thinking. She offers a "microbe centered" view of life that provides stimulating thinking and insights into the complex way living systems interact.

Lewis Thomas

Research pathologist Lewis Thomas has written several essay collection books reflecting his years as a scientist. You may wish to look up *The Lives of a Cell* (Viking Press, 1974), *Late Night Thoughts Listening to Mahler's Symphony* (Viking Press, 1983), and *The Fragile Species* (Charles Scribner's Sons, 1992).

William H. Calvin

William Calvin is another medical scientist (neuroscientist) with several good essay-style books to his credit: *The Throwing Madonna, Essays on the Brain* (McGraw-Hill, 1983) and *The River That Flows Uphill, a Journey from the Big Bang to the Big Brain* (Sierra Club Books, 1986) are two good ones.

Mathematics

Paul Hoffman

The Man Who Loved Only Numbers (Hyperion, 1998): An excellent biography of mathematician, Paul Erdös.

Charles Seife

Zero: The Biography of a Dangerous Idea (Viking, 2000): Shows how the concepts of zero and infinity can radically impact human civilizations and philosophy.

Clute and Nicholls in *The Encyclopedia of Science Fiction* (1995) report that a surprising number of science fiction writers are either mathematicians or trained in the field, including Arthur C. Clarke, Donald Kingsbury, Larry Niven, Rudy Rucker, Vernor Vinge, David Zindell, and others. Refer to Chapter 9 for classroom activities and ideas.

Earth Science/Paleontology

Peter Ward

Peter Ward is a professor of geological science at the University of Washington, Seattle. One of his recent titles, *Future Evolution, an Illuminated History of Life to Come* (W. H. Freeman, 2001), uses evolutionary principles to extrapolate future life after it passes through the needle's eye of extinction events during our present era. Ward alludes to an earlier book on the same theme by **Dougal Dixon** called *After Man, a Zoology of the Future* (St. Martin's Press, 1981), but Ward takes a more optimistic view of human survival into that future. Dixon does look at human evolution over the next five million years in *Man after Man, An Anthropology of the Future*

(St. Martin's Press, 1990). Any of these books could provide an entertaining way to discuss paleontology and evolution.

Brad Matsen/Ray Troll (illustrator)

Planet Ocean, a Story of Life, the Sea, and Dancing to the Fossil Record (Ten Speed Press, 1994) is a kid-friendly approach to paleontology containing a unique odyssey of discovery elements and entertaining drawings.

John McPhee

Annals of the Former World (Farrar, Strauss, & Giroux, 1998): includes *Basin and Range* and *Rising from the Plains,* two excellent books on the geology of the American west. McPhee is an elegant writer, not to be missed.

Tim Flannery

The Eternal Frontier, an Ecological History of North America and Its Peoples (Atlantic Monthly Press, 2001).

Simon Winchester

The Map That Changed the World (HarperCollins, 2001) tells the beginnings of geology as a science through the life and struggles of William Smith, a workingman who spent his life creating a geological map of England. Smith was the first man to read the record of past times through the sedimentary rock record. *Krakatoa: The Day the World Exploded, August 27, 1888* (Harper-Collins, 2003) demonstrates how this volcanic event of global magnitude jump-started many scientific disciplines and demonstrates that we live in an interdependent and interconnected world.

At least two paleontologists of note have attempted some science fiction of their own. **Robert Bakker**, the long-haired proponent of "hot-blooded" dinosaurs, wrote *Raptor Red* (Bantam, 1995), a novel about the life and times of a female Utahraptor 120 million years ago. **George Gaylord Simpson**, considered one of the greatest paleontologists of the twentieth century, wrote *The Dechronization of Sam Magruder* (St. Martin's Press, 1996), about a middle-aged scientist thrown back 80 million years into the past, struggling to survive and find meaning in his life as the only representative of his species in a strange world.

Miscellaneous Books of Merit

The Seven Daughters of Eve (W. W. Norton & Co., 2001) by Bryan Sykes.
Sykes proposes that all modern European and North American Caucasian populations can be traced back to seven women who lived during Ice Age times.

Powers of Ten (Scientific American Books, 1982) by Philip and Phylis Morrison.

Dinosaurs to Diatoms, the Size and Scale of Living Things (Island Press, 1994) by Chris McGowan.

The Measure of the Universe (Harper & Row, 1983) by Isaac Asimov.
The books by the Morrisons, McGowan, and Asimov show how and why size and scale matter to living things.

The Cartoon History of the Universe, Volumes 1–7, from the Big Bang to Alexander the Great (Doubleday, 1990) by Larry Gonick and *The Cartoon History of the Universe II, Volumes 8–13, from the Springtime of China to the Fall of Rome* (Doubleday 1994). Gonick also wrote, with Mark Wheelis, *The Cartoon Guide to Genetics* (Barnes & Noble Books, 1983). The cartoon guides are fun and visual scientific resources.

A SAMPLING OF SCIENCE RESOURCES FOR YOUNGER STUDENTS AND/OR RELUCTANT READERS

The books listed above should serve both your needs and those of better readers or older students. Younger students and/or reluctant readers may need a gentler introduction to science topics. Below I've listed a small selection of such science titles and a few authors who specialize in science for the elementary-grade-levels. Basic references also tend to be more visual and make no assumptions about previous knowledge, so they are great for teachers who consider themselves neophytes in certain topics.

Physical Sciences

Cartoon Guide to Physics (HarperPerennial, 1992) by Larry Gonick.

There Are No Electrons: Electronics for Earthlings (Clearwater Publishing Co., 1991) by Kenn Amdahl, a quirky and funny introduction to electronics.

Earth and Space Sciences

Mary Anning, the Fossil Hunter (Silver Press, 1998), a picture book by Dennis Frandin with illustrations by Tom Newsom about one of the earliest fossil hunters.

The Dinosaurs of Waterhouse Hawkins (Scholastic, 2001) by Barbara Kerley, illustrated by Brian Selznick, details the lifework of the paleoartist who created some of the first dinosaur models for the Crystal Palace in England's Hyde Park.

Asteroid Impact (Dial Books, 2000) and *Dinosaur Tree* (Aladdin Paperbacks, 1999) by Doug Henderson, an excellent writer as well as artist.

Jack Horner Living with Dinosaurs (W. H. Freeman Co., 1994), written by Don Lessem and illustrated by Janet Hamlin.

Find the Constellations (Houghton Mifflin, 1976) by H. A. Rey is a good introduction to stargazing.

Moonwalk: The First Trip to the Moon (Random House Books for Young Readers, 1989) by Judy Donnelly, illustrated by Dennis Davidson, skillfully recreates the excitement and wonder of the *Apollo 11* expedition to the moon.

Martian Fossils on Earth? The Story of Meteorite ALH 84001 (Millbrook Press, 1997) by Fred Bortz outlines in exciting detail how scientists track down the origins of rocks from space.

Life Sciences/Nature

Arnosky's Ark (National Geographic, 1999), *Field Trips: Bug Hunting, Animal Tracking, Bird-Watching, Shore Walking* (HarperCollins, 2002), and *Nearer Nature* (HarperCollins, 1996) by Jim Arnosky, an artist–turned writer. His website (http://www.jimarnosky.com) features interactive activities for children and ideas for teachers.

One Small Square Backyard by Donald M. Silver, illustrated by Patricia J. Wynne (W. H. Freeman, 1993) provides a good resource for encouraging careful observation and "thinking small" when looking for wonders in your own backyard.

The Case of the Mummified Pigs and Other Mysteries in Nature (Boyds Mills Press, 1995) by Susan E. Quinlan, illustrated by Jennifer Owings Dewey.

Dinosaurs in the Garden (Plexus Publications, 1988) by Gary Raham provides an evolutionary perspective for understanding the lives of common backyard creatures.

Math and Miscellany

Tiger Math (2000) and *Chimp Math* (2002) by Ann Nagda explores mathematical concepts using animals in the Denver Zoo.

The Grapes of Math: Mind-Stretching Math Riddles (Scholastic, 2001), *The Best of Times: Math Strategies That Multiply* (2002), and *Math for All Seasons: Mind-Stretching Math Riddles* (2002) by Greg Tang. All three titles are illustrated by Harry Briggs.

A Street through Time, a 12,000 Year Walk through History (DK Publishing, 1998) is an excellent picture book with elaborate two-page spreads showing a human community as it transforms from settlement to metropolis. Ann Millard provides the text. Illustrator Steve Noon places a time traveler in each picture, forcing the reader to pay close attention to detail.

EXPERT RESOURCES

How to Reach Them

Don't shrink from contacting scientific experts if you need the latest information on a particular topic. But don't waste their time either by asking them to bring you up-to-date on the last ten years of research in a field. Do your homework first and selectively target your questions and requests. You will find, for the most part, that the experts are eager to share what they know and reaching them is easier than you might think. Try the following:

- Find the human resources available from local natural history museums through volunteer newsletters or public program announcements.

- Check out the faculty at nearby universities. Many of them will be happy to share their expertise with the public at large and especially with the extended educational community.

- Hikes or volunteer opportunities with local conservation organizations will allow you to network with many people who have specialized knowledge.

- Network with other science teachers through professional organizations like NSTA (National Science Teachers Association). Some of your colleagues will already be using science fiction to teach science fact.

- Government agencies often provide surprisingly good services. Look up www.usgs.org, for example; they have a feature called "Ask USGS" where geologists will answer your specific questions by e-mail on virtually any Earth-science-related topic.

- Use your favorite search engine and look up "scientific organizations." You will find links to organizations in every science field.

- If you find a particularly useful book, go in search of the author. You may be able to reach him through his publisher or under a personal Web site. You may also be able to find the author through professional writers' associations. For example, at the National Association of Science Writers, Inc. Web site (www.nasw.org/) you can link to the Web pages of individual members. For writers who specialize in writing for children, see the reference to SCBWI in the following section.

Enticing Experts into the Classroom

Local experts who work for government or university agencies may offer their time gratis as a public service. Some will be better presenters than others, either through experience or by inclination. You can often get a feel for how a given person might be after speaking with him or her for a short time.

Many published authors enjoy public speaking and the opportunity to promote their books as well as educate children. A large selection can be reached through the Society of Children's Book Writers and Illustrators (SCBWI), an international organization based in Los Angeles. If you go to their Web site at www.scbwi.org you can find links to the various regional chapters. Contact regional advisors to find authors and illustrators creating books in your area of interest. There are usually fees for programs offered, but the quality of presentations is high and they can often be targeted to your special concerns.

Keeping the facts and the fictions straight is something of a scientific quest in itself and reinforces the premise that both science and science fiction explore mysterious wonders. Hopefully, the research that allows you to distinguish the "what if" from the "what is" will also spark you to transmit the sense of wonder inherent in both disciplines to your students.

APPENDIX 2

Categories of National Science Content Standards

Grades 5–8	Grades 9–12

1. **Science as inquiry standards:**
   Abilities necessary to do scientific inquiry   Abilities necessary to do scientific inquiry
   Understanding about scientific inquiry   Understanding about scientific inquiry

2. **Physical science standards:**
   Properties and changes of properties   Structure of atoms
   in matter   Structure and properties of matter
   Motions and forces   Chemical reactions
   Transfer of energy   Motions and forces
       Conservation of energy and increase in disorder
       Interactions of energy and matter

3. **Life science standards:**
   Structure and function in living systems   The cell
   Reproduction and heredity   Molecular basis of heredity
   Regulation and behavior   Biological evolution
   Populations and ecosystems   Matter, energy, and organization in living systems
   Diversity and adaptations of organisms   Behavior of organisms

4. **Earth and space science standards:**
   Structure of the Earth system   Energy in the Earth system
   Earth's history   Geochemical cycles
   Earth in the solar system   Origin and evolution of the Earth system
       Origin and evolution of the universe

5. **Science and technology standards:**
   Abilities of technological design   Abilities of technological design
   Understanding about science and technology   Understanding about science and technology

6. **Science in personal and social perspectives:**
   Personal health   Personal and community health
   Populations, resources, and environments   Population growth
   Natural hazards   Natural resources
   Risks and benefits   Environmental quality
   Science and technology in society   Natural and human-induced hazards
       Science and technology in local, national, and global challenges

7. **History and nature of science standards:**
   Science as a human endeavor   Science as a human endeavor
   Nature of science   Nature of scientific knowledge
   History of science   Historical perspectives

8. **Unifying concepts and processes standard** (which all other standards incorporate):
   Systems, order, and organization
   Evidence, models, explanation
   Change, constancy, and measurement
   Evolution and equilibrium
   Form and function

APPENDIX 3

List of Activities and Suggested Grade Levels

Chapter 6: Physical Sciences

Using *Mission of Gravity* by Hal Clement
   Suggested activities dealing with inclined planes, force and motion, simple machines, force and fluid pressure, meteorology, light and optics, and aerodynamics.

   Age levels: middle school to high school

Using the short story, "giANTS" by Edward Bryant
   • Creating artificial insects (size and scale problem)

   Age levels: 4th to 8th grade

Using *Collapsium* by Wil McCarthy
   • Collapsium and crystals
   • Wellstone and the periodic table

   Age levels: 9th to 12th grade

Demonstration: gold, silver, and relativity
   Age levels: 9th to 12th grade

Chapter 7: Earth and Space Sciences

Using *The Deep Time Diaries* by Gary Raham
   • Writing and illustrating personal deep time diaries

   Age levels: 6th to 8th grade

Using various resources
   • Alien-building
   • World-building

   Age levels: 5th grade to high school

Chapter 8: Life Sciences

Using *Dune* by Frank Herbert

- Drawing the sandworm life cycle

- Comparing sandworm to earthworm biology

- Speculations on sandworm sex

- Sketching stillsuits; inventing new features for stillsuits based on desert adaptations of Earth creatures.

- Making a Fremen phrase book

Age levels: 6th to 12th grade

Using various resources from movies, novels, and short stories

- Put an artificial intelligence on trial for being human

Age levels: 6th to 12th grade

Using various "first contact" novels and short stories

- Calculating your value for the Drake Equation

Age levels: 9th to 12th grade

Chapter 9: Across Spacetime and the Curriculum

Using various time travel novels and stories

- Writing a "what if?" story

- Making an alternate history timeline

- Making a technology timeline spanning the student's life

Age levels: 6th to 12th grade

Using Louise Engdahl's "Federation" novels

- Comparing Federation policy with cultural contacts on Earth

Age levels: 9th to 12th grade

- Analyzing trash from an alien's viewpoint

Age levels: 5th to 12th grade

Using *Flatland* by Edwin Abbott

- Creating a model of Flatland

- Making a Flatland board game

- Designing public buildings in Flatland

- Describing invasions from Spaceland

Age levels: 8th to 10th grade

APPENDIX 4

Curriculum Developed around The Deep Time Diaries, **Written and Illustrated by the Author**

Science Reading Guide, Outline, Rubric, and Vocabulary Sheet
developed by Vicky Jordan,
Wellington Junior High, Wellington, CO

The Deep Time Diaries **Reading Guide**

1. **Deep Time** (Transcriber's Introduction)
   a. What is deep time?

   b. Using relative dating techniques, write the letters of the rock layers shown below in order from oldest to youngest.

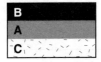

   c. Common fossils found only in certain rock layers are called_____.

   d. Absolute dating allows scientists to know the age of a certain rock layer. It works because in nature, certain_____ elements decay into more stable ones by throwing off parts of their_____. The time it takes half of a radioactive element to change into something else is called its_____.

   > i. If you want to measure the age of something that is only a few thousand years old, what would be the best "atomic clock" to use?

   > ii. If you want to measure the age of something that is millions of years old, what is an "atomic clock" you could use?

2. **Fossilization** (Teratorns and Tar Pits)
   a. What exactly is a fossil? (Use the glossary)

   b.

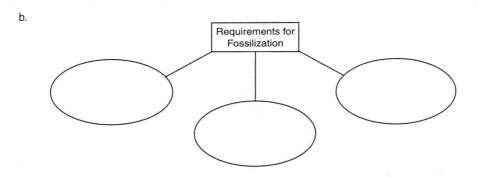

Way to fossilhood:	What happens during this process?	What things can get fossilized this way?
Freeze-dry (freezing or mummification)		
Sap-sicle (amber)		
Get petrified (petrification)		
Get carbonized (carbonization)		
Casts		
Molds		
Trace fossils		

3. **Living fossils** are organisms that exist in present time and have not changed much since prehistoric times. As you read *The Deep Time Diaries*, find examples of living fossils that the Olifees saw during different time periods.

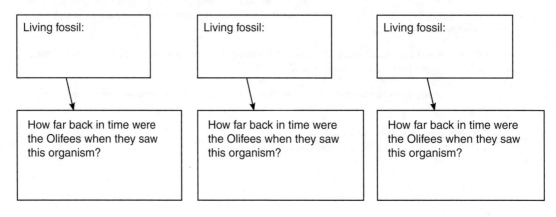

Living fossil:	Living fossil:	Living fossil:
How far back in time were the Olifees when they saw this organism?	How far back in time were the Olifees when they saw this organism?	How far back in time were the Olifees when they saw this organism?

4. Some organisms that the Olifees saw during their time travels have since gone extinct. Find three organisms that the Olifees saw in different time periods that have gone extinct.

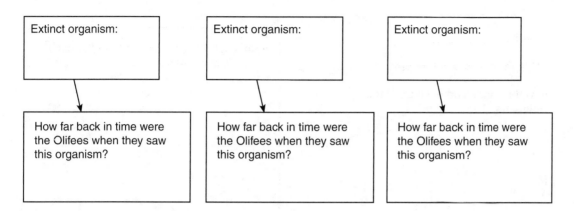

Extinct organism:	Extinct organism:	Extinct organism:
How far back in time were the Olifees when they saw this organism?	How far back in time were the Olifees when they saw this organism?	How far back in time were the Olifees when they saw this organism?

5. Use the diagrams of the Earth found at the end of each time jump to draw how the continents looked during the time periods shown below:

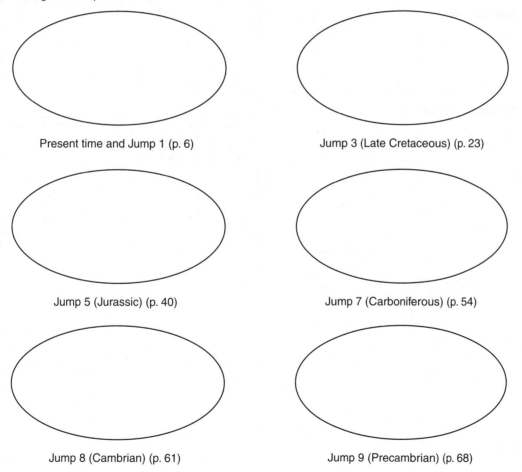

Present time and Jump 1 (p. 6)

Jump 3 (Late Cretaceous) (p. 23)

Jump 5 (Jurassic) (p. 40)

Jump 7 (Carboniferous) (p. 54)

Jump 8 (Cambrian) (p. 61)

Jump 9 (Precambrian) (p. 68)

Notes for your own journal entries: As you read *The Deep Time Diaries*, take notes on the time period that you will be writing about for your own journal.

Era: _____

Period: _____

Millions of years before present: _____

Draw the shape and position of the continents:

Geological events:

Animals: Look for living fossils and animals that have gone extinct.

Environmental conditions:

Other notes:

Plants: Look for living fossils and plants that have gone extinct.

Origins and Extinctions of Various Life Forms through Geological Time

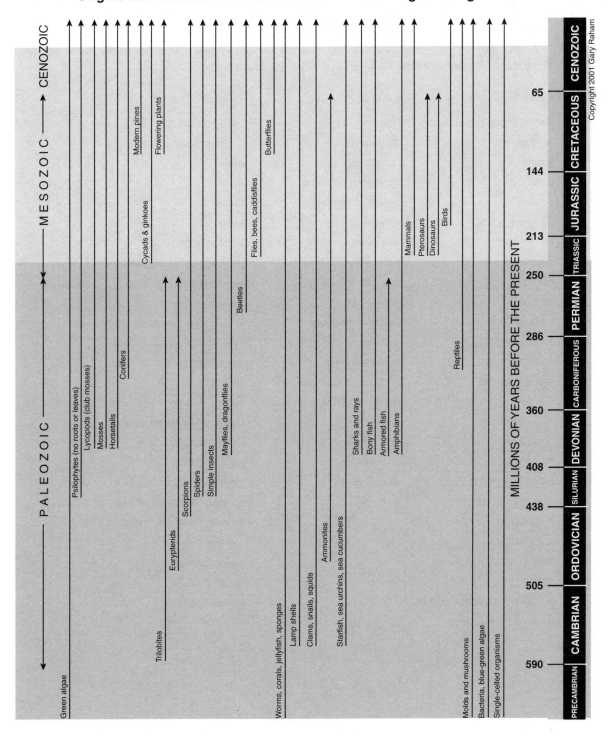

THE DEEP TIME DIARIES

Scientific Vocabulary

Words that you may choose to use in context in your diary. There are many more, so don't think this is a complete list! This will just help you brainstorm.

Level 1	Level 2	Level 3
geology/geological time	igneous	ossified skeleton
reptile	metamorphic	cartilaginous skeleton
mammal	sediments	niche
coral	deposit/deposition	flora
conifer	evolution/evolve	fauna
flowering plant	vertebrate	saline
consumer	invertebrate	amniote egg
carnivore	cephalopod	protozoan/protist/plankton
herbivore	mollusk	genus/genera
omnivore	adaptation	species
predator/prey	rock names (basalt	desiccation/desiccate
food chain	sandstone, granite, etc.)	aerodynamic/streamlined
cold-blooded	metamorphosis	vascular plants
warm-blooded	body parts: antennae,	rhizome
larvae	thorax, abdomen, segments	locomotion (types of animal movement)
vegetation	habitat	Pangaia/Gondwanaland
organism	peat	radiometric dating
fossil/fossilization	competition	relative dating
paleontologist	filter-feeder	spore/sporangia
photosynthesis	arthropod	specific details about plant or animal
respiration		anatomy that use scientific terms
camouflage		ectothermic
extinct/extinction		endothermic
marine		angiosperm
all plant and animal names		gymnosperm
all time period names		

English Reading Guide

Developed by Mark Barnes, Wellington Junior High, Wellington, CO

Introduction

1. Summarize what is known about *The Deep Time Diaries*.

_____

_____

_____

_____

2. What is a transcriber?

_____

_____

3. What are some things the author does in the first few pages to make the book seem realistic?

_____

_____

_____

_____

4. Does the author directly say, "Neesha talks too much?" No, he lets us know that by having Jon say, "Neesha's still finding enough oxygen somewhere to babble all the time." And he doesn't tell us "Neesha annoys Jon." Instead, he shows us examples of her annoying Jon and we can figure it out from there. So with things like that in mind, **explain how the author communicates to us what Jon and Neesha are like.**

_____

_____

_____

_____

5. Now that you have explained the author's description techniques, list below your conclusions. What do you know about Jon and Neesha's personalities? Starting with the introduction section, but adding details as you read all of *The Deep Time Diaries,* describe these two time travelers. (Words and phrases are okay.)

Jon Olifee: *Neesha Olifee:*

Jumps 1–3

1. At the start of Jump 1, what **simile** is used to describe Earth?

_____

_____

2. Explain why the Florida peninsula would have "looked more like a fat thumb than a finger."

_____

_____

3. List three examples of sensory details—other than sight. (Also, state which sense it appeals to.)
    1.
    2.
    3.

4. In the scene with "Old Gimp," list the example of **personification**.

_____

_____

5. Find the great **"opener"** at the bottom of page 12. Write the sentence here. Which "opener" is used?

_____

_____

6. What **simile** is used to describe the big palm fronds on page 13?

_____

_____

7. Page 13, third paragraph (starts with "Then I forgot . . ."). List at least five **strong action verbs** found in this paragraph.

_____

_____

8. Page 20, Day 2 entry by Jon. List 3 **quality adjectives**, 2 **strong action verbs**, 1 "ly" **adverb**, and 1 **clause word**.

Q.A.s (3) _____   clause word (1): _____

S.A.V.s (2): _____   "ly" (1): _____

Jumps 4–6

1. Page 27, Day 1 entry by Neesha. List three **strong action verbs** and three **quality adjectives**.
S.A.V.s (3): _____

Q.A.s (3): _____

2. Page 28, Day 3 entry by Jon. List the **simile** in the first paragraph and circle the two things being compared.

_____

_____

3. Page 35, Day 1 entry by Neesha. List the two "ly" **adverbs** in this entry and the words they describe. Then star the one that is used as an **opener**.

_____

_____

4. How is **personification** used to describe the movement of the flood waters?

_____

_____

5. Page 42, Day 2 entry by Neesha. List the two **prepositional openers** she uses in this entry.

_____

_____

6. In Jon's final entry of this section, find the sentence that gives us more insight into **Neesha's character**, specifically related to her being very talkative.

_____

_____

Jumps 7–9

1. Page 49, Day 1 entry by Neesha. List 5 **strong action verbs** in this entry.

_____

_____

2. What is the **simile** that is used to describe how the oversized dragonflies flew around Jon?

_____

_____

3. Page 50, Day 2 entry by Jon. Write one **adjective opener** and one **prepositional opener** from this entry.

_____

_____

4. Page 56, Day 1 entry by Jon. List 5 quality **adjectives** from this entry.

_____

_____

5. Find two **similes** on page 58.

_____

_____

6. Page 63, Day 1 entry by Neesha. Find three **clausal openers** in this entry.

_____

_____

7. **Summarize** who the Caretaker is and why the time machine was built.

_____

_____

_____

_____

YIKES! WHERE DO I START?

Five Steps to a Creative Story:
by Gary Raham

1. **Decide on your main characters—give them a résumé.**
   Name? Age? Sex? Hair color? Size? Favorite colors? Best friend? Boyfriend/girlfriend? Favorite food? Pet peeves? Talky or quiet? Looks? Etc.

2. **Give your characters a consistent voice.**
   Do they speak in complete sentences or fragments? Are they whiny or decisive? Are they wishy-washy? Do they have a lisp? Do they use big words or get words mixed up? Etc.

3. **Create a believable, accurate setting.**
   (Yes, that's what research is for!)
   Make a list of animals and plants in the environment. Which ones are dangerous? What's the weather like? Are there seasons? Any natural disasters that could happen?

4. **Get your characters in trouble.**
   (It's more fun that way.) Get them lost. Chase them with big, ugly creatures. Have a flood, earthquake, volcanic eruption, asteroid strike, etc. Have them do something stupid. Let them have a fight with another character. Use the dramatic situation to help illustrate the time and place setting for the reader.

5. **Get them out of trouble by their own actions.**
   Maybe characters' "faults" will work to their benefit. Maybe they learn something to solve a problem. Maybe they act bravely under pressure. Maybe they learn to ask for help from a friend.

Other Tips:

- Use active verbs and nouns. Avoid lots of adjectives and adverbs.

- Every sentence should accomplish several things: character development, moving the plot, setting the scene. Leave out wimpy sentences that just fill space.

- Close your eyes and visualize each scene. Then you can just report what you see!

Index

About the Author

Gary Raham is a freelance science writer and illustrator who has published in a variety of markets for both children and adults. He has written for *Cricket, Highlights for Children, Read, Writing!,* and Discovery Channel Books and has five book titles to his credit—including *The Deep Time Diaries,* a time travel adventure used to teach Earth science and creative writing in several Colorado schools. His video script *Fossils: Uncovering Clues to the Past* won an Award of Excellence at the Denver Video Festival in 1993 and he received the Colorado Author's League Top Hand Award for his nonfiction in 2001.

Gary taught high school and junior high science for two years before pursuing his writing and illustrating interests, and science education remains a strong interest. While serving a term as the Regional Advisor for the Rocky Mountain Chapter of the Society for Children's Book Writers and Illustrators he helped encourage writers and illustrators to share their talents with children. He is also a member of the Guild of Natural Science Illustrators and Science Fiction Writers of America.

Gary enjoys hiking with his wife, Sharon, in the Colorado Rockies. He also hunts fossils with other amateur paleontologists, leads sketching hikes as a Master Naturalist for the city of Fort Collins, and enjoys tennis and nature photography.